easy knitting
Babies & Children

7

easy knitting
Babies &
Children

30 projects to make for your home and to wear

Consultant: Nikki Trench

hamlyn

An Hachette UK Company
www.hachette.co.uk

First published in Great Britain in 2013 by
Hamlyn, a division of Octopus Publishing Group Ltd
Endeavour House
189 Shaftesbury Avenue
London
WC2H 8JY
www.octopusbooks.co.uk

ISBN 978-0-600-62755-5

A CIP catalogue record for this book is available from the
British Library

Printed and bound in China

10 9 8 7 6 5 4 3 2 1

Contents

Introduction

If you can knit a few basic stitches, you can create stylish items for babies and children to wear or use, to brighten the nursery and to give as gifts.

Whether you are a relative beginner, a confident convert or a long-term aficionado, there are projects here to delight. While your first attempts may be a bit uneven, a little practice and experimentation will ensure you soon improve. None of the projects here is beyond the scope of even those fairly new to the hobby.

A home-made keepsake for a new arrival or special child trumps many a store-bought gift. Choose one to make from the delightful range here: clothes (cardigans, hats and slippers, for example), blankets and throws, toys or decorative items for nurseries and bedrooms. All would make charming, unique gifts.

Knitting essentials

All you really need to get knitting is a pair of needles and some yarn. For some projects, that's it; for others additional items are required, most of which can be found in a fairly basic sewing kit. All measurements are given in metric and imperial. Choose which to work in and stick with it since conversions may not be exact.

• **Needles** These come in metric (mm), British and US sizes and are made from different materials, all of which affect the weight and 'feel' of the needles – which you choose is down to personal preference. Circular and double-pointed needles are sometimes used as well.

• **Yarns** Specific yarns are listed for each project, but full details of the yarn's composition and the ball lengths are given so that you can choose alternatives, either from online sources or from your local supplier, many of whom have very knowledgeable staff. Do keep any leftover yarns (not forgetting the ball bands, since these contain vital information) to use for future projects.

• **Additional items**: Some projects require making up and finishing, and need further materials or equipment, such as sewing needles, buttons and other accessories. These are detailed in each project's Getting Started box.

What is in this book

All projects are illustrated with several photographs to show you the detail of the work – both inspirational and useful for reference. A full summary of each project is given in the Getting Started box so you can see exactly what's involved. Here, projects are graded from one ball of yarn (straightforward, suitable for beginners) through two (more challenging) to three balls (for knitters with more confidence and experience).

Also in the Getting Started box is the size of each finished item, yarn(s), needles and additional items needed, and what tension/gauge the project is worked in. Finally, a breakdown of the steps involved is given so you know exactly what the project entails before you start.

At the beginning of the pattern instructions is a key to all abbreviations that are used in that project, while occasional notes expand on the pattern instructions where necessary.

If you have enjoyed the projects here, you may want to explore the other titles in the Easy Knitting series: *Chic, Cosy, Country, Vintage & Retro* and *Weekend*. For those who enjoy crochet, a sister series, Easy Crochet, features similarly stylish yet simple projects.

Metric	British	US
2 mm	14	0
2.5 mm	13	1
2.75 mm	12	2
3mm	11	n/a
3.25 mm	10	3
3.5 mm	n/a	4
3.75 mm	9	5
4 mm	8	6
4.5 mm	7	7
5 mm	6	8
5.5 mm	5	9
6 mm	4	10
6.5 mm	3	10.5
7 mm	2	n/a
7.5 mm	1	n/a
8 mm	0	11
9 mm	0	13
10 mm	0	15

Baby sweater and hat

This is a great present for the baby who has everything — his very own designer knit.

Soft yarn with an element of cashmere makes this cable-patterned sweater and beanie hat snug and glamorous.

The Yarn

Debbie Bliss Baby Cashmerino is perfect for babies with its ultra-soft mix of pure wool, cashmere and microfibre so that it can be washed at low temperatures – essential for baby items. There is a fantastic colour range that includes all the traditional pastel shades as well as interesting contemporary colours.

GETTING STARTED

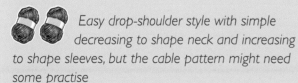 *Easy drop-shoulder style with simple decreasing to shape neck and increasing to shape sleeves, but the cable pattern might need some practise*

Size:

SWEATER To fit chest: *41[46:51:56]cm/16[18:20:22]in*

Actual width: *48.5[53:58:64]cm/19[20¾:22¾:25¼]in*

Length from shoulder: *24[28:32:38]cm/9½[11:12½:15]in*

Sleeve seam: *15[17:20:24]cm/6[6¾:8:9½]in*

HAT All round width: *38[38:40:40]cm/15[15:15¾:15¾]in*

Note: *Figures in square brackets [ ] refer to larger sizes; where there is only one set of figures, it applies to all sizes*

How much yarn:

Sweater *3[4:5:6] x 50g (2oz) balls of Debbie Bliss Baby Cashmerino, approx 125m (137 yards) per ball*

Hat *1 x 50g (2oz) ball of Debbie Bliss Baby Cashmerino, approx 125m/137 yards per ball*

Needles:

Pair of 3mm (no. 11/US 2) knitting needles

Pair of 3.75mm (no. 9/US 5) knitting needles

Additional items:

Cable needle

Stitch holder

2 buttons for sweater

Tension/gauge:

28 sts and 30 rows measure 10cm (4in) square over patt on 3.75mm (no. 9/US 5) needles

IT IS ESSENTIAL TO WORK TO THE STATED TENSION/ GAUGE TO ACHIEVE SUCCESS

What you have to do:

Work cable pattern. Decrease stitches to shape neck. Make simple buttonhole. Increase stitches to shape sleeves. Pick up stitches around neck to work neckband.

Abbreviations:

alt = alternate;
cm = centimetre(s);
cont = continue;
dec = decrease(ing);
inc = increase(ing);
C4F = cable 4 front by slipping next 2 sts on to cable needle and leaving at front of work, k2, then k 2 sts from cable needle;
foll = follow(s)(ing);
k = knit;
m1 = make one stitch by picking up loop lying between needles and working into back of it;
p = purl; **patt** = pattern;
psso = pass slipped stitch over;
rem = remain(ing);
rep = repeat;
RS = right side; **sl** = slip;
st(s) = stitch(es);
st st = stocking/stockinette stitch;
tog = together;
WS = wrong side;
yfwd = yarn forward/yarn over between needles to make a st.

Instructions

SWEATER:
BACK:

With 3mm (no. 11/US 2) needles cast on 53[59:65:71] sts. Beg with a k row, work 7 rows in st st.

Next row: (WS) P2[5:4:4], m1, (p3, m1, p4, m1) 7[7:8:9] times, p2[5:5:4]. 68[74:82:90] sts.

Change to 3.75mm (no. 9/US 5) needles. Cont in patt as foll:

1st row: (RS) K0[3:1:0], p2[2:2:1], *k4, p2, rep from * to last 0[3:1:5] sts, k0[3:1:4], p0[0:0:1].

2nd and 4th rows: P0[3:1:0], k2[2:2:1], *p4, k2, rep from * to last 0[3:1:5] sts, p0[3:1:4], k0[0:0:1].

3rd row: K0[3:1:0], (p2, C4F), 0[0:1:0] times, p2[2:2:1], *k4, p2, C4F, p2, rep from * to last 6[9:1:5] sts, k4[4:1:4], p2[2:0:1], k0[3:0:0].

5th and 6th rows: As 1st and 2nd rows.** These 6 rows form patt. Cont in patt until work measures 24[28:32:38] cm/9½[11:12½:15]in from 4th row on st st roll edge, ending with a WS row.

Next row: Patt 1[4:4:3], patt 2tog, (patt 2, patt 2tog, patt 3, patt 2tog) 7[7:8:9] times, patt 2[5:4:4]. 53[59:65:71] sts.

Change to 3mm (no. 11/US 2) needles.

Next row: P17[18:20:23], turn and work on these sts for shoulder band. Leave rem 36[41:45:48] sts on a st holder.

Shoulder band:

Beg with a k row, work 4 rows in st st. Cast/bind off loosely purlwise.

With WS facing, sl centre 19[23:25:25] sts on a st holder for back neck, rejoin yarn to rem 17[18:20:23] sts and cast/bind off purlwise.

FRONT:

Work as given for Back to **. Cont in patt until work measures 19[19:19:21] rows shorter than Back to right shoulder, ending with a WS row.

Shape neck:

Next row: Patt 30[31:34:38] sts, turn and work on these sts for the first side of neck. Leave rem 38[43:48:52] sts on a st holder. Dec 1 st at neck edge on next 3[5:5:5] rows, then on 5[4:4:4] foll alt rows. 22[22:25:29] sts. Work 4[4:4:6] rows straight, ending with a WS row.

Next row: (Patt 0[0:2:2], patt 0[0:2:2] tog) 0[0:2:3] times, (patt 2[3:3:3], patt 2tog) 5[4:3:3] times, patt 2. 17[18:20:23] sts.

Change to 3mm (no. 11/US 2) needles. P 1 row.

Buttonhole row: K9[9:10:12], yfwd, k2tog, k6[7:8:9].

Work 4 rows in st st. Cast off purlwise.

With RS facing, sl centre 8[12:14:14] sts on a st holder for front neck, rejoin yarn to rem 30[31:34:38] sts and patt to end.

Dec 1 st at neck edge on next 3[5:5:5] rows, then on 5[4:4:4] foll alt rows. 22[22:25:29] sts. Work 4[4:4:6] rows straight, ending with a WS row.

Next row: (RS) Patt 2, (patt 2tog, patt 2[3:3:3]) 5[4:3:3] times, (patt 0[0:2:2]tog, patt 0[0:2:2]) 0[0:2:3] times. 17[18:20:23] sts. Cast/bind off.

SLEEVES:

With 3mm (no. 11/US 2) needles cast on 35[35:37:39] sts. Beg with a k row, work 7 rows in st st.

Next row: P1[1:3:4], m1, (p4[4:3:3], m1) 8[8:10:10] times, p2[2:4:5]. 44[44:48:50] sts.

Change to 3.75mm (no. 9/US 5) needles. Cont in patt as foll:

1st row: (RS) K0[0:2:3], p2, *k4, p2, rep from * to last 0[0:2:3] sts, k0[0:2:3].

2nd and 4th rows: P0[0:2:3], k2, *p4, k2, rep from * to last 0[0:2:3] sts, k0[0:2:3].

3rd row: K0[0:2:3], p2, k4, p2, (C4F, p2, k4, p2) 2[2:3:3] times, (C4F, p2) 1[1:0:0] times, k4[4:2:3], p2[2:0:0].

5th row: Inc in first st, k0[0:1:2], p1[1:2:2], *k4, p2, rep from * to last 6[6:2:3] sts, k4[4:0:1], inc in next st, k1. 46[46:50:52] sts.

6th and 8th rows: P1[1:3:4], *k2, p4, rep from * to last 3[3:5:0] sts, k2[2:2:0], p1[1:3:0].

7th row: K1[1:3:0], p2[2:2:0], (k4, p2) 1[1:1:0] times, *C4F, p2, k4, p2, rep from * to last 1[1:3:4] sts, (C4F) 0[0:0:1] times, k1[1:3:0].

9th row: Inc in first st, k0[0:2:3], p2, *k4, p2, rep from * to last 7[7:3:4] sts, k4[4:1:2], p1[1:0:0], inc in next st, k1[1:1:0], p0[0:0:1]. 48[48:52:54] sts.

Cont as set, inc 1 st at each end of 0[7:7:4] foll 4th rows to 48[62:66:62] sts, then at each end of 4[0:1:5] foll 6th rows. 56[62:68:72] sts.

Cont without shaping until Sleeve measures 15[17:20:24] cm/6[6¾:7¾:9½]in from 4th row on roll cuff edge, ending with a WS row.

Shape top:
Cast/bind off 7[8:9:10] sts at beg of the next 4 rows. 28[30:32:32]sts.
Cast/bind off 8[9:10:10] sts at beg of the next 2 rows. Cast/bind off rem 12 sts.

NECKBAND:
Join right shoulder seam.
With 3.75mm (no. 9/US 2) needles and RS facing, pick up and k4 sts along shoulder button band, 15[15:15:17] sts down left front neck, work across front neck sts as foll: patt 3, patt 2tog, patt 3[2:3:3], patt 0[2:2:2]tog, patt 0[3:4:4], pick up and k15[15:15:17] sts up right front neck, then k across 19[23:25:25] back neck sts from holder, then pick up and k4 sts along shoulder button band. 64[71:75:79] sts. P 1 row.

Buttonhole row: (RS) K3, yfwd, k2tog, k to end. Work 5 rows in st st. Cast/bind off loosely.

BEANIE HAT:
With 3mm (no. 11/US 2) needles cast on 83[83:89:89] sts. Beg with a k row, work 7 rows in st st.

Next row: P3[3:6:6], m1, (p3, m1, p4, m1) 11 times, p3[3:6:6]. 106[106:112:112] sts.

Change to 3.75mm (no. 9/US 5) needles. Cont in patt as foll:

1st row: K1[1:4:4], *p2, k4, rep from * to last 3[3:0:0] sts, p2[2:0:0], k1[1:0:0].

2nd row and foll alt rows: P1[1:4:4], *k2, p4, rep

* to last 3[3:0:0] sts, k2[2:0:0], p1[1:0:0].

3rd row: K1[1:4:4], *p2, C4F, p2, k4, rep from * to last 9[9:0:0] sts, p2[2:0:0], (C4F, p2, k1) 1[1:0:0] times.

5th row: As 1st row.

7th row: As 3rd row.

Cont as set until work measures 12[13:14:15] cm/4¾[5:5½:6]in from beg of cable patt on roll edge, ending with a WS row.

Shape crown:

1st row: K1[1:0:0], p2[2:0:0], *sl 1, k1, psso, k2tog, p2, rep from * to last 1[1:4:4] sts, (sl 1, k1, psso, k2tog) 0[0:1:1] times, k1[1:0:0]. 72[72:74:74] sts.

2nd and 4th rows: P1[1:0:0], k2[2:0:0], *p2, k2, rep from * to last 1[1:2:2] sts, p1[1:2:2].

3rd row: K1[1:0:0], p2[2:0:0], *k2, p2, rep from * to last 1[1:2:2] sts, k1[1:2:2].

5th row: K1[1:0:0], p2[2:0:0], *k2tog, p2, rep from * to last 1[1:2:2] sts, (k2tog) 0[0:1:1] times, k1[1:0:0]. 55 sts.

6th row: P1, *k2, p1, rep from * to end.

7th row: K1, *p2tog, k1, rep from * to end. 37 sts.

8th row: P1, *k1, p1, rep from * to end.

9th row: K1, (k2tog) 18 times. 19 sts.

Cut off yarn, leaving a long end. Thread cut end through rem sts, draw up tight and fasten off securely.

Stalk:
With 3mm (no. 11/US 2) needles cast on 6 sts. Work 6 rows in st st. Cast/bind off.

Making up

SWEATER:
Overlap front shoulder band over back shoulder band and secure at side edge. Insert markers 11[12:13:14]cm/4¼[4¾:5¼:5½]in down from shoulders on back and front. Placing centre of sleeve top to shoulder seam, sew in sleeves between markers. Join side and sleeve seams, reversing seam on roll edges. Sew on buttons.

BEANIE HAT:
Join back seam of hat, reversing seam on roll edge. Join cast-on and cast/bound-off edges of stalk, then attach the stalk to the top of the hat.

Alphabet blocks

Combine your knitting skills with some foam blocks to create these fun cubes that will give hours of play.

Big and bold, toddlers and small children will have fun with these colourful nursery cubes worked in a variety of stitches and textures.

The Yarn

Sirdar Snuggly DK is a hard-wearing mixture of 55% nylon and 45% acrylic that is ideal for the rough and tumble of children's playtime. There is a large choice of colours, from traditional baby pastels to contemporary brights.

GETTING STARTED

 Each cube consists of mainly easy panels of simple patterns although letter panels are worked using the intarsia technique

Size:
Each cube is 20cm x 20cm x 20cm (8in x 8in x 8in)

How much yarn:
2 x 50g (2oz) balls of Sirdar Snuggly DK, approx 165m (180 yards) per ball, in each of the following five colours A, B, C, D and E
1 ball in colour F

Needles:
Pair of 3.75mm (no. 9/US 5) knitting needles

Additional items:
3 x 19cm (7½in) cubes of foam, All-purpose glue 60cm (24in) of polyester wadding/batting, 150cm (60in) wide

Tension/gauge:
22 sts and 28 rows measure 10cm (4in) square over st st on 3.75mm (no. 9/US 5) needles
IT IS ESSENTIAL TO WORK TO THE STATED TENSION/ GAUGE TO ACHIEVE SUCCESS

What you have to do:
Make six separate squares for each cube, varying stitches and designs on each square as follows: One square in single colour reverse stocking/stockinette stitch; one square in single colour moss/seed stitch; one square in striped stocking/stockinette stitch; two squares in stocking/stockinette stitch with letters knitted in using intarsia technique and one base square in striped zig-zag pattern. Cover foam cubes with wadding/ batting. Make up knitted cubes leaving bases open. Stretch knitted cubes over foam and sew bases in position.

Instructions

Abbreviations:
beg = beginning; **cm** = centimetre(s); **cont** = continue; **foll** = follow(s)(ing); **k** = knit; **p** = purl; **patt** = pattern; **rep** = repeat; **RS** = right side; **st(s)** = stitch(es); **st st** = stocking/stockinette stitch; **tog** = together; **WS** = wrong side

Note: When working letters from charts, read odd-numbered (RS) rows from right to left and even-numbered (WS) rows from left to right. Use small, separate balls of yarn for each area of colour and twist yarns tog on WS of work when changing colour to avoid holes forming. Where appropriate over a few sts only, strand colour not in use across WS of work.

CUBE: (With letters A and B)
Side 1:
With C, cast on 45 sts. Beg with a p row, work 58 rows in reverse st st.
Cast/bind off.

7th row: K2 E, (1 B, 7 E) to last 3 sts, 1 B, 2 E.
8th row: With E, p to end.
Rep these 8 rows 5 times more, using a different colour for contrast zig-zag on each rep. Cast/bind off.

CUBE: (With letters C and D)
Side 1:
With B, cast on 45 sts. Beg with a p row, work 58 rows in reverse st st. Cast/bind off.
Side 2:
With A, cast on 43 sts.
Next row: K1, (p1, k1) to end.
Rep this row to form moss/seed st until work measures 20cm/8in from beg. Cast/bind off in patt.
Side 3:
With D, cast on 45 sts. Beg with a k row, cont in st st and stripe patt as foll: 10 rows D, 2 rows F, 10 rows E, 2 rows F, 10 rows C, 2 rows F, 10 rows B, 2 rows F, 10 rows E. Cast/bind off with E.
Side 4:
With C, cast on 45 sts.
Beg with a k row, cont in st st and foll chart 3, working letter C in colours D and A. Cast/bind off.
Side 5:
With E, cast on 45 sts.
Beg with a k row, cont in st st and foll chart 4, working letter D in colour C. Cast/bind off.
Base:
With D, cast on 45 sts. Work 48 rows in zig-zag patt as given for Cube (with letters A and B), using colours randomly for each rep. Cast/bind off.

CUBE: (With letters E and F)
Side 1:
With D, cast on 45 sts. Beg with a p row, work 58 rows in reverse st st. Cast/bind off.
Side 2:
With E, cast on 43 sts.
Next row: K1, (p1, k1) to end.
Rep this row to form moss/seed st until work measures 20cm (8in) from beg. Cast/bind off in patt.
Side 3:
With A, cast on 45 sts.
Beg with a k row, cont in st st and stripe patt as foll:
10 rows A, 2 rows each E, D and C, 10 rows A, 2 rows each D, B and C, 10 rows A, 2 rows each B, E and C,

Side 2:
With B, cast on 43 sts.
Next row: K1, (p1, k1) to end.
Rep this row to form moss/seed st until work measures 20cm (8in) from beg. Cast/bind off in patt.
Side 3:
With B, cast on 45 sts.
Beg with a k row, cont in st st and stripe patt as foll:
8 rows B, 2 rows A, 8 rows E, 2 rows A, 8 rows C, 2 rows A, 8 rows D, 2 rows A, 8 rows B, 2 rows A and 8 rows E. Cast/bind off with E.
Side 4:
With A, cast on 45 sts.
Beg with a k row, cont in st st and foll chart 1, working letter A in colour E. Cast/bind off.
Side 5:
With D, cast on 45 sts. Beg with a k row, cont in st st and foll chart 2, working letter B in colours A and F. Cast/bind off.
Base:
With E, cast on 45 sts. Cont in zig-zag patt as foll, stranding colour not in use loosely across WS of work:
1st row: (RS) With E, k to end.
2nd row: With E, p to end.
3rd row: K6 E, 1 B, (7 E, 1 B) to last 6 sts, 6 E.
4th row: P5 E, 1 B, 1 E, (1 B, 5 E, 1 B, 1 E) to last 6 sts, 1 B, 5 E.
5th row: (K1 B, 3 E) to last st, 1 B.
6th row: P1 E, (1 B, 1 E, 1 B, 5 E) to last 4 sts, (1 B, 1 E) twice.

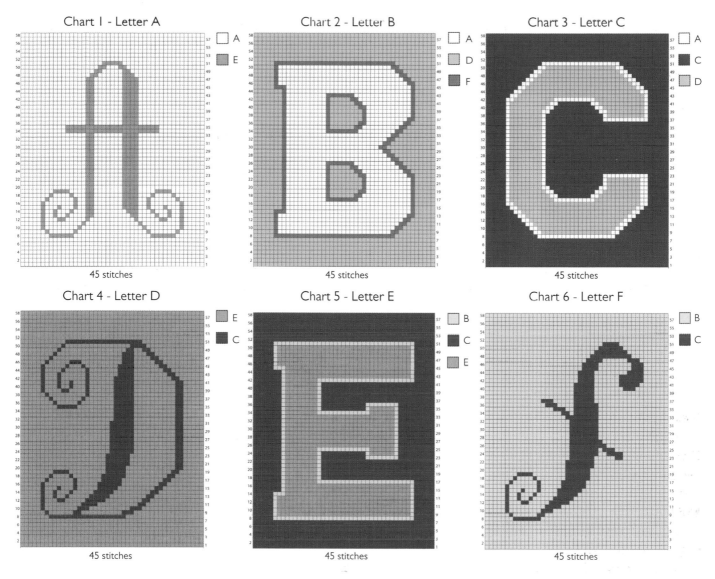

Chart 1 - Letter A
45 stitches
☐ A
◼ E

Chart 2 - Letter B
45 stitches
☐ A
☐ D
◼ F

Chart 3 - Letter C
45 stitches
☐ A
◼ C
☐ D

Chart 4 - Letter D
45 stitches
◼ E
◼ C

Chart 5 - Letter E
45 stitches
☐ B
◼ C
◼ E

Chart 6 - Letter F
45 stitches
☐ B
◼ C

10 rows A. Cast/bind off with A.

Side 4:

With 3.75mm (no. 9) needles and C, cast on 45 sts. Beg with a k row, cont in st st and foll chart 5, working letter E in colours E and B. Cast off.

Side 5:

With B, cast on 45 sts.

Beg with a k row, cont in st st and foll chart 6, working letter F in colour C. Cast/bind off.

Base:

With F, cast on 45 sts. Work 48 rows in zig-zag patt as given for Cube (with letters A and B), using colours randomly for each rep. Cast/bind off.

 Making up

Join Sides 1, 2, 3 and 4 of a cube to form an open circle, then stitch striped Side 5 piece into top of open circle, matching corners accurately, to form an open cube.

Cut 18 x 19cm (7½in) squares of wadding/batting. Using a little glue, stick wadding/batting to sides of foam cubes and leave to dry. Insert a foam cube into open end of knitted cube and stretch to fit. Position base in place and, using mattress st, sew in base (note that base is slightly shorter than sides to allow for stretching sides to fit). Repeat for remaining cubes.

Child's shrug

Tiny and fashionable, this snug shrug is a party must for any girl.

Finish this fitted shrug with frilled cuffs and a garter-stitch edging to the front.

GETTING STARTED

 Some increasing to shape sleeves and hen attaching band around neck and front edge

Size:

To fit chest: *61[66:71]cm/24[26:28]in or 3–4 [5–6: 7–8] years*

Actual width: *64[69:74]cm/25[27:29]in*

Length from shoulder: *21[23:25]cm/8¼[9:10]in*

Sleeve seam: *18[22:27]cm/7[8¾:10¾]in*

Note: *Figures in square brackets [ ] refer to larger sizes; where there is only one set of figures, it applies to all sizes*

How much yarn:

You will need 2[3:3] x 50g (2oz) balls of Sirdar Snuggly Pearls DK, approx 170m (186 yards) per ball

Needles:

Pair of 3.25mm (no.10/US 3) knitting needles
Pair of 4mm (no.8/US 6) knitting needles

Additional items:

Stitch holder

Tension/gauge:

22 sts and 28 rows measure 10cm (4in) square over st st on 4mm (no. 8/US 6) needles
IT IS ESSENTIAL TO WORK TO THE STATED TENSION/GAUGE TO ACHIEVE SUCCESS

What you have to do:

Work in stocking/stockinette stitch (st st). Increase stitches to shape sleeves. Work sleeves and fronts separately, leave stitches on holder, then join up with extra cast-on stitches for back. Work front band in garter stitch (g st).

The Yarn

This yarn is a nylon and acrylic mixture with tiny glittery strands so it has a slight sparkle. You could look for a similar yarn from a different manufacturer, but check the ball band to make sure it is knitted with 4mm (no. 8/US 6) needles.

Instructions

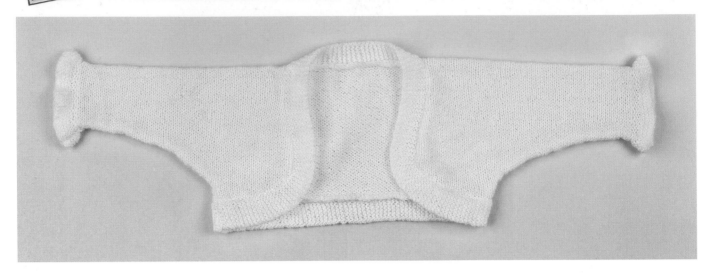

Abbreviations:

alt = alternate;
beg = beginning;
cm = centimetre(s);
cont = continue;
dec = decrease;
foll = following;
g st = garter stitch (every row knit);
inc = increase(ing);
k = knit;
m1 = make one stitch by picking up loop lying between needles and knitting into back of it;
RS = right side;
st(s) = stitch(es);
st st = stocking/stockinette stitch

Note: Back and Fronts are worked in one piece.

LEFT FRONT:

With 4mm (no. 8/US 6) needles cast on 12[14:16] sts. Beg with a k row, cont in st st.

Work 6[8:11] rows, casting on 4 sts at end (front edge) on 3rd row, then inc one st at the same edge on next 3[5:8] rows. 19[23:28] sts.

Shape sleeves:

1st and 2nd sizes only: Work 3[2] rows, inc one st at each end of every row. 25[27] sts.

3rd size only: Work 1 row. 28 sts.

All sizes: Work 7[10:12] rows, inc one st at side edge on every row. 32[37:40] sts. Work 1 row.

Cast on 4[6:10] sts at side edge on next and 1[0:0] foll alt row. 40[43:50] sts. Work 1 row.

1st size only: Cast on 4 sts at side edge and dec one st at front edge on next row. 43 sts.

2nd and 3rd sizes only: Cast on 6[10] sts at side edge and dec one st at front edge on next and foll alt row. 53[68] sts.

All sizes: Work 1 row. Cast on 12 sts at side edge on next row and dec 0[0:1] st at front edge. 55[65:79] sts. Work 1[1:3] rows, then dec one st at front edge on next and 3 foll 4th rows. 51[61:75] sts. Work 10[12:12] rows straight.

Back neck: Work 3 rows, inc one st at neck edge on every row. 54[64:78] sts. Cut off yarn and leave sts on a holder.

RIGHT FRONT:

Work as given for Left Front, reversing shapings.

BACK:

With RS of work facing, rejoin yarn at side edge on Left Front, k across 54[64:78] sts on holder, cast on 30[32:34] sts for back neck, then with RS of work facing, k across 54[64:78] sts. Right Front sts on holder. 138[160:190] sts.

Work 22[24:26] rows in st st.

Shape sleeves: Cast/bind off 12 sts at beg of next 2 rows. 114[136:166] sts. Cast/bind off 4[6:10] sts at beg of foll 6 rows. 90[100:106] sts. Dec one st at each end of next 10[12:12] rows. 70[76:82] sts.

Work 5[7:11] rows straight. Cast/bind off.

Cuffs: (Work 2 alike)

With 3.25mm (no. 10/US 3) needles and RS of work facing, pick up and k 30[34:38] sts along cuff edge of Sleeve.

Next 3 rows: Knit to end.

Next row: K2, (m1, k2) to end. 44[50:56] sts.

Next row: Knit to end.
Next row: K2, (m1, k2) to end. 65[74:83] sts.
Next 4 rows: Knit to end. Cast/bind off.

Using backstitch, join cast-on and cast/bound-off edges of band together. Placing band seam at right side seam, sew band in place around edges, again using backstitch.

 ## Making up

Pressing:
Press gently using a damp cloth and a warm iron.
Joining the seams:
Join side and sleeve seams using backstitch.
Front band:
With 3.25mm (no. 10/US 3) needles cast on 8 sts. Cont in g st until band is long enough to fit around front and back edges. Pin band in place as you are working and take care not to stretch it around front curves.
Cast/bind off.

Introducing Mr Ted

Meet Mr Ted, the fun-to-knit teddy with his own stylish wardrobe. He's soft and round and quite irresistible.

This traditional teddy couldn't be easier to make. From nose to toes, he's worked in one basic stitch. Simple shaping gives him his soft, round shape and there is little sewing up to do too. Fill him with bean-bag beads for even more cuddle appeal.

The Yarn

The weight and pure wool fibre content of Debbie Bliss Rialto is perfect for making soft toys, and it can be hand washed if necessary. There are several 'bear shades' available and plenty of colour choice for teddy's clothes.

GETTING STARTED

 Worked throughout in garter stitch with easy increasing and decreasing for shaping

Size:

Toy is approximately 28cm (11in) in height

How much yarn:

2 x 50g (2oz) balls of Debbie Bliss Rialto in main colour, approx 105m (115 yards) per ball

1 ball in contrasting colour A

1 ball in contrasting colour B and oddments of grey

Needles:

Pair of 3.75mm (no. 9/US 5) knitting needles

Additional items:

2 small grey buttons for eyes

3 small horn-effect buttons for waistcoat

Polyester toy stuffing

Approximately 100g (3½oz) polystyrene bean-bag beads

Small funnel

Long yarn needle

Tension/gauge:

24 sts and 48 rows measure 10cm (4in) square over garter stitch on 3.75mm (no. 9/US 5) needles

IT IS ESSENTIAL TO WORK TO THE STATED TENSION/ GAUGE TO ACHIEVE SUCCESS

What you have to do:

Work in garter stitch (every row knit). Work simple increasing and decreasing for shaping. Work turning rows for shaping. Take care with sewing up and stuffing the bear so that he is a good shape.

 # Instructions

Abbreviations:

alt = alternate; **dec** = decrease(ing);

foll = follow(s)(ing); **inc** = increase(ing); **k** = knit;

m 1 = make 1 st by picking up horizontal strand lying between needles and k into back of it;

rem = remain(ing); **rep** = repeat; **RS** = right side;

st(s) = stitch(es); **tbl** = through back of loop(s);

tog = together; **yon** = yarn over needle.

BEAR BODY: (Worked in one piece from neck)

With main colour, cast on 12 sts.

Next row: K twice in every st. K1 row.

Rep last 2 rows once. 48 sts. K12 rows.

Next row: (K10, k twice in next 4 sts, k10) twice. K3 rows.

Next row: (K11, k twice in next 2 sts, k2, k twice in next 2 sts, k11) twice. 64 sts

K30 rows.

Next row: K12, (k2tog tbl) 4 times, k24, (k2tog) 4 times, k12. K1 row.

1st turning row: K9, turn, yon, k9.

2nd turning row: K across all sts, working yon tbl with next st. Rep last 2 rows once.

Next row: K10, (k2tog tbl) 4 times, k20, (k2tog) 4 times, k10.

Work 2 turning rows twice.

Next row: K8, (k2tog tbl) 4 times, k16, (k2tog) 4 times, k8. K1 row.

Next row: K6, (k2tog tbl) 4 times, k12, (k2tog) 4 times, k6. 32 sts. K1 row.

Next row: *K2tog, rep from * to end.

Cast/bind off rem 16 sts.

Join centre back and bottom seam. Insert funnel through opening in top and fill body with bean-bag beads to 1cm (½in) from top. Fill top of body firmly with toy stuffing. Run a thread around top and pull up tightly to secure stuffing.

HEAD:

With main colour, cast on 21 sts. K2 rows.

Next row: (RS) K10, m1, k1, m1, k10. K1 row.

Next row: K11, m1, k1, m1, k11. K1 row.

Cont to inc in this way on every RS row until there 27 sts. Now inc 1 st at either side of centre st on every row, AT THE SAME TIME inc 1 st at each end of next and every foll 4th row until there are 47 sts. Keeping centre straight, cont to inc at sides on every 4th row as set until there are 53 sts. K1 row. Dec 1 st at each end of next and foll 2 alt rows. 47 sts. K1 row.

**Next 2 rows: K2tog, k19, turn, yon, k to end.

Next 2 rows: K2tog, k13, turn, yon, k to end.

Next 2 rows: K2tog, k7, turn, yon, k to end.

Next row: K2tog, k to end, working yon tog with next st as you come to them.**

Rep from ** to **. Cast/bind off 17 sts at beg of next 2 rows. 5 sts. K10 rows. Inc 1 st at each end of next and every foll alt row until there are 15 sts.

K11 rows. Dec 1 st at each end of next and every foll 4th row until there are 7 sts and then at each end of foll 6th row. 5 sts. Work 3 rows. Cast/bind off.

Sew seams on top and back of head and stuff firmly. Sew two small grey buttons to either side of head.

EARS: (Make 2)

With main colour, cast on 15 sts. K8 rows.

Next row: K2, (k2tog, k1) 3 times, k2tog, k2. K1 row.

Next row: K2, (k2tog, k1) 3 times. Cast/bind off.

Sew cast-on edge of ears securely to top and sides of head as shown in photograph.

NOSE:

With selected oddment, cast on 5 sts. K1 row. Dec 1 st at each end of next 2 rows. Fasten off rem st, leaving a long end. Sew nose to front of head. Use remaining end of yarn at point to work one straight stitch and two downwards diagonal stitches for mouth.

LEGS: (Make 2)

With main colour, cast on 34 sts. K6 rows.

Shape foot:

Next row: (RS) K15, k2tog tbl, k2tog, k15. K1 row

Next row: K14, k2tog tbl, k2tog, k14. K1 row.

Next row: K13, k2tog tbl, k2tog, k13. K1 row.

Next row: K8, (k2tog tbl) 3 times, (k2tog) 3 times, k8. 22 sts. K3 rows.

Next row: K10, k twice in next 2 sts, k10. K9 rows.

Next row: K11, k twice in next 2 sts, k11. K9 rows.

Next row: K12, k twice in next 2 sts, k12. K9 rows. 28 sts

Next row: K2tog, k10, k2tog tbl, k2tog, k10, k2tog. K1 row.

Next row: K2tog, k8, k2tog tbl, k2tog, k8, k2tog. K1 row.

Next row: K2tog, k6, k2tog tbl, k2tog, k6, k2tog. K1 row.
Next row: *K2tog, rep from * to end. Cast/bind off rem 8 sts.

SOLES:

With main colour, cast on 3 sts. K1 row. Inc 1 st at each end of next and every foll alt row to 9 sts. K11 rows. Dec 1 st at each end of next and every foll alt row to 3 sts. Cast/bind off.

ARMS: (Make 2)

With main colour, cast on 6 sts.
Next row: K twice in each st. K1 row.
Rep last 2 rows once. 24 sts. K14 rows.
Next row: K10, k2tog tbl, k2tog, k10. K1 row.
Next row: K9, k2tog tbl, k2tog, k9. K1 row.
Next row: K8, k2tog tbl, k2tog, k8. K3 rows.
Next row: K7, k twice in next 4 sts, k7.
Next row: K9, k twice in next 4 sts, k9. 26 sts. K21 rows.
Next row: K2tog, k9, k2tog tbl, k2tog, k9, k2tog. K1 row.
Next row: K2tog, k7, k2tog tbl, k2tog, k7, k2tog. K1 row.
Next row: K2tog, k5, k2tog tbl, k2tog, k5, k2tog. K1 row.
Next row: *K2tog, rep from * to end.
Cast/bind off rem 7 sts.

Making up

Sew head securely to top of body. Join centre back and lower seams on legs and arms, leaving top shaped edge open. Sew soles onto base of feet. Insert funnel into opening and fill limbs with bean-bag beads until 1cm (½in) from top. Stuff remainder of limbs with toy stuffing and close openings. Using a long needle, sew legs onto sides of body, to align with lower side shaping. Work through the centre of one leg, 1cm (½in) from top, pass needle through body and through corresponding point on second leg. Pass needle through the legs and body in this way three or four times. Fasten yarn off securely. Sew on arms in same way.

SCARF:

With contrasting colour B, cast on 75 sts. K9 rows. Cast/bind off knitwise. Cut 10 × 8cm (3in) lengths of yarn. Fold in half and knot 5 on each end of scarf for fringe. Trim the fringe.

WAISTCOAT:

With contrasting colour A, cast on 70 sts. K24 rows, making buttonholes on 5th, 13th and 21st rows as foll:
Buttonhole row: K to last 2 sts, yon, k2tog.
Right front:
Next row: K18, turn and cont on these sts only for right front.
****Next row:** Cast/bind off 3 sts for armhole, k to end.
Dec 1 st at each end of next and foll 3 alt rows.
K1 row.
Keeping armhole edge straight, dec 1 st at front edge on next and every foll 4th row until 3 sts rem.
K2 rows. Cast/bind off.
Back:
Rejoin yarn to rem sts, cast/bind off 3 sts, k31 including st used to cast/bind off, turn and cont on these sts for back.
Next row: Cast/bind off 3 sts, k to end.
Dec 1 st at each end of next and foll 3 alt rows. Work straight until back matches Right front to shoulder. Cast/bind off.
Left front:
Rejoin yarn to rem 18 sts and complete to match Right front from ** to end.
Join shoulder seams and sew on buttons.

Funky striped throw

Bold, chunky and tough, this throw is perfect for a kid's room where it can go on the bed or join in the fun and games.

Cheerful stripes of bright, variegated colours are the focal point of this chunky throw worked in strips of stocking/stockinette stitch.

GETTING STARTED

 Chunky yarn knits up quickly and the three-strip construction makes this a good project for a beginner

Size:
Throw measures approximately 120cm x 150cm (47in x 59in)

How much yarn:
25 x 50g (2oz) balls of Sirdar Indie, approx 43m (47 yards) per ball, in main colour A
16 balls in contrast colour B
19 balls in contrast colour C

Needles:
Pair of 10mm (no. 000/US 15) knitting needles

Additional items:
8mm (no. 0/US L11) crochet hook

Tension/gauge:
8.5 sts and 12 rows measure 10cm (4in) square over st st on 10mm (no. 000/US 15) needles
IT IS ESSENTIAL TO WORK TO THE STATED TENSION/GAUGE TO ACHIEVE SUCCESS

What you have to do:
Work each strip in stocking/stockinette stitch following stripe sequence given in instructions. Cut off yarn after each stripe and join in the new colour. Darn in ends neatly afterwards. Sew strips together to form throw. Work crochet edging around outer edge.

The Yarn
Sirdar Indie contains 49% acrylic and 51% wool. The practicality of man-made fibres and the good looks of wool combine to produce a good-quality fabric that is warm yet lightweight. The yarn is available in colourful, variegated shades.

Instructions

Abbreviations:
beg = beginning;
cm = centimetre(s);
cont = continue;
foll = follows; **k** = knit;
patt = pattern;
RS = right side;
st(s) = stitch(es);
st st = stocking/
stockinette stitch

THROW:
Left-hand strip:
With A, cast on 35 sts. Beg with a k row, cont in st st,
working in stripe patt
as foll:
20 rows A; 10 rows B; 10 rows A; 20 rows C; 20 rows B; 50
rows A; 20 rows C; 10 rows B and 20 rows A.
Cast/bind off with A.

Centre strip:
With B, cast on 35 sts. Beg with a k row, cont in st st,
working in stripe patt
as foll:
10 rows B; 10 rows A; 50 rows C; 30 rows B; 10 rows A; 10
rows C; 10 rows B; 30 rows A and 20 rows C.
Cast/bind off with C.

Right-hand strip:
With A, cast on 35 sts. Beg with a k row, cont in st st,
working in stripe patt
as foll:
10 rows A; 10 rows C; 20 rows B; 10 rows A; 30 rows C;
10 rows A; 10 rows B; 30 rows A; 20 rows B; 10 rows C; 10
rows A and 10 rows B. Cast/bind off with B.

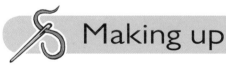

Making up

Darn in all ends neatly. Join three strips to form one large
panel. With 8mm (no. 0/US L11) crochet hook, A and
with RS of work facing, work in double (US single) crochet
around outer edge of throw. Fasten off.

HOW TO
CROCHET THE EDGES

Use an 8mm (no.0/US L11) crochet hook and yarn A to make the crochet border around each edge of the throw.

1 Working on the right side of the fabric, insert the hook through from front to back under the first stitch along the edge. Wrap the yarn around the hook and pull a loop back through to the front of the fabric.

3 Wrap the yarn around the hook and pull through both loops on the hook to complete the crochet stitch. Repeat steps 2 and 3 working a crochet stitch into each stitch along the edge.

2 Take the hook back through the fabric in the next stitch. Catch the yarn with the hook and pull a loop back through to the front. You will have two loops on the hook.

4 At each corner, work three crochets stitches into the same stitch to turn the corner.

Baby's hooded top and shoes

Easy stitches and very little shaping make this the perfect beginner's project.

Worked in stocking/stockinette stitch and simple textured patterns, this hooded top and matching shoes are great accessories for groovy babies.

The Yarn

Sublime Baby Cashmere Merino Silk DK is a mixture of 75% extra fine merino wool, 20% silk and 5% cashmere. This blend of natural fibres is delicately soft and smooth next to a baby's skin. It can be hand washed and there is a choice of 10 adorable baby shades.

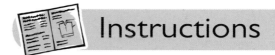 Instructions

Abbreviations:

alt = alternate; **beg** = beginning; **cm** = centimetre(s); **cont** = continue; **dec** = decrease(ing); **foll** = follow(s)(ing); **k** = knit; **m1** = make one stitch by picking up strand lying between needles and knit into back of it; **p** = purl; **patt** = pattern; **psso** = pass slipped stitch over; **rem** = remain(ing); **rep** = repeat; **RS** = right side; **sl** = slip; **st(s)** = stitch(es); **st st** = stocking/stockinette stitch; **tog** = together; **WS** = wrong side

GETTING STARTED

 Easy stitch patterns and hooded top requires hardly any shaping

Sizes:

To fit ages: 3–6[6–9:9–12] months
To fit chest: 46[48:51]cm/18[19:20]in
Actual size chest: 55[57:59]cm/21½[22½:23½]in
Length: 26[27.5:29]cm/10[10¾:11½]in
Shoes to fit ages: 0–6[6–12] months
Note: Figures in square brackets [ ] refer to larger sizes only; where there is only one set of figures, it applies to all sizes

How much yarn:

4[4:4] x 50g (2oz) balls of Sublime Baby Cashmere Merino Silk DK, approx 116m (127 yards) per ball

Needles:

Pair of 3.75mm (no. 9/US 5) knitting needles
Pair of 4mm (no. 8/US 6) knitting needles
Spare 4mm (no. 8/US 6) knitting needle

Additional items:

Stitch holder and stitch markers
1 medium shell button for top
2 small shell buttons for shoes

Tension/gauge:

22 sts and 28 rows measure 10cm (4in) square over st st on 4mm (no. 8/US 6) needles
IT IS ESSENTIAL TO WORK TO THE STATED TENSION/ GAUGE TO ACHIEVE SUCCESS

What you have to do:

Work hem and slit edgings in moss/seed stitch, with main fabric in stocking/stockinette stitch. Work simple textured pattern for yoke, dividing work at centre for opening on front. Pick up stitches around neck to work hood. Make two patch pockets and sew on. Make shoes with soles in moss/seed stitch and instep in stocking/ stockinette stitch. Make moss/seed stitch strap and fasten with button across instep.

HOODED TOP:
BACK:
With 4mm (no. 8) needles cast on 61[63:65] sts.
1st row: (RS) K1, (p1, k1) to end.
Rep this row to form moss st.
Work 3 more rows, ending with a WS row.
Next row: Moss/seed st 3, k to last 3 sts, moss/seed st 3.
Next row: Moss/seed st 3, p to last 3 sts, moss/seed st 3.
Rep last 2 rows 4 times more. Beg with a k row, cont in st st until work measures 16[17:18] cm/6¼[6¾:7]in from beg, ending with a WS row.
Next row: (RS) P to end.
Next row: K to end.
Work in yoke patt as foll:
Next row: (RS) P1, k1, p1, k2[3:4], p1, k1, p1, (k3, p1, k1, p1) to last 5[6:7] sts, k2[3:4], p1, k1, p1.
Next row: P1, k1, p4[5:6], k1, (p5, k1) to last 6[7:8] sts, p4[5:6], k1, p1.*
The last 2 rows form patt. Rep them until work measures 26[27.5:29]cm/10¼[10¾:11½]in from beg, ending with a WS row.
Shape shoulders and back neck:
Keeping patt correct, cast/bind off 5 sts at beg of next 2 rows. 51[53:55] sts.
Next row: Cast/bind off 5 sts, patt until there are 11[11:12]
sts on right-hand needle, turn and complete this side of neck first.
Next row: Cast/bind off 5 sts, patt to end.
Cast/bind off rem 6[6:7] sts.
With RS of work facing, rejoin yarn to rem sts, cast/bind off centre 19[21:21] sts, patt to end. Cast/bind off 5 sts at beg of next 2 rows. Cast/bind off rem 6[6:7] sts.

FRONT:
Work as given for Back to *.
The last 2 rows form patt. Rep them until work measures 19[20.5:22]cm/7½[8:8¾]in from beg, ending with a WS row.
Divide for neck opening:
Next row: (RS) Patt 32[33:34] sts, turn and complete this side of opening first. Keeping patt correct, work straight until opening measures 7cm (2¾in) from beg, ending with a WS row.
Shape shoulder:
Cast/bind off 5 sts at beg of next and foll alt row, then

6[6:7] sts at beg of next alt row. Work 1 row on rem 16[17:17] sts. Cut off yarn and leave sts on a holder. With RS of work facing, rejoin yarn to rem sts, cast on 3 sts, p1, k1, p1 across these 3 sts, patt to end. 32[33:34] sts. Work straight until opening measures same as first side, ending with a RS row.
Shape shoulder:
Cast/bind off 5 sts at beg of next and foll alt row, then 6[6:7] sts at beg of next alt row. Do not cut off yarn as this will be used for hood, leave rem 16[17:17] sts on needle.

HOOD:
Join shoulder seams, matching patt carefully.
With 4mm (no. 8/US 6) needles, using yarn left at right front neck edge and with RS of work facing, p1, k1, p1, k13[14:14] sts of right front, pick up and k27[29:29] sts around back neck placing a marker on centre st (30th[32nd:32nd] of sts on right-hand needle so far), then k13[14:14], p1, k1, p1 across sts of left front. 59[63:63] sts.
Keeping 3 sts at each front in moss/seed st and rem sts in st st, work 7 rows, ending with a WS row.
Next row: (RS) Patt to marked st, m1, k1, m1, patt to end. Rep last 8 rows once more. 63[67:67] sts. Work straight until hood measures 19[20:20]cm/7½[8:8]in from beg,

ending with a WS row.

Next row: Patt to within 2 sts of marked st, sl 1, k1, psso, k1, k2tog, patt to end.

Work 1 row. Rep last 2 rows twice more, dec 1 st at centre of last WS row. 56[60:60] sts.

Next row: (RS) Patt 28[30:30], turn, fold hood in half with WS facing and needles tog and, using spare 4mm (no. 8/US 6) needle, cast/bind off sts from each needle tog to form seam.

BUTTON LOOP:

With 4mm (no. 8/US 6) needles cast on 14 sts. Cast/bind off.

POCKETS: (Make 2)

With 4mm (no. 8/US 6) needles cast on 16 sts.

1st row: (K1, p1) to end.

2nd row: (P1, k1) to end.

Rep last 2 rows once more. Beg with a k row, cont in st st until pocket measures 7cm (2¾in) from beg. Cast/bind off.

SHOES: (Make 2)

With 3.75mm (no. 9/US 5) needles cast on 29[33] sts.

1st row: P1, (k1, p1) to end.

Rep this row 3 times more to form moss/seed st. Beg with a k row, cont in st st until work measures 5.5cm (2 in) from beg, ending with a WS row.

Shape instep:

Next row: K19[22], turn.

Next row: P9[11] turn.

Beg with a k row, work 16[18] rows in st st on these 9[11] sts only. Cut off yarn. With RS facing, rejoin yarn at base of instep and pick up and k 10[11] sts along side of instep, k across 9[11] sts of instep, pick up and k 10[11] sts along other side of instep, k rem 10[11] sts. 49[55] sts.

Next row: P1, (k1, p1) to end.

Rep last row 8[10] times more.

Shape sole:

Next row: (RS) Moss/seed st 29[33], turn.

Next row: Moss/seed st 9[11], turn.

Next row: Moss/seed st 8[10], work 2tog, turn.

Rep last row until 6[7] sts rem on each side of centre sts of sole.

Next row: Moss/seed st 3[4], work 2tog, moss/seed st 3[4], work2tog, moss/seed st 2[3], work 2tog, moss/seed st 1, turn.

Next row: Moss/seed st 11[14], work 2tog, moss/seed st

2[3], work 2tog, moss/seed st 1.

Cast/bind off rem 16[20] sts in moss/seed st.

STRAPS: (Make 2)

With 3.75mm (no. 9/US 5) needles cast on 16[18] sts.

1st row: (P1, k1) to end.

2nd row: (K1, p1) to end.

Cast/bind off in moss/seed st.

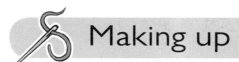

Making up

HOODED TOP:

Join side seams from above moss/seed st slits to beg of yoke patt. Sew cast-on sts at base of front opening behind base of left front band. Fold button loop in half and sew both ends behind left front opening at halfway point. Sew on button to correspond with loop. Sew pockets to front approximately 3.5cm (1½in) from lower edge and 3.5cm (1½in) from side seams.

SHOES:

Sew heel and centre back seam of each shoe. Sew one end of strap to top edge of moss/seed st at left side of one shoe and right side of the other, then sew on a small button to opposite end of strap and through shoe so that button is on outer side of each shoe when worn.

Funky coin purse

Small but perfectly formed, this purse has an added flower, tassels and a twizzle!

Striped in four colours, this purse is a bright and cheerful accessory that has plenty of add-on interest.

The Yarn

Debbie Bliss Cotton DK contains 100% cotton. It is a good-looking yarn that is available in plenty of contemporary shades for striking colour work.

GETTING STARTED

 Easy pattern if instructions are followed carefully but constructing decorations requires patience

Size:
Purse is approximately 13.5cm x 10cm (5½in x 4in)

How much yarn:
1 x 50g (2oz) ball of Debbie Bliss Cotton DK, approx 84m (92 yards) per ball, in each of the following colours A, B, C and D

Needles:
Pair of 3mm (no. 11/US 2) knitting needles
Pair of 4mm (no. 8/US 6) knitting needles

Additional items:
Crochet hook
Zip fastener to fit in turquoise
Red sewing thread and needle

Tension/gauge:
20 sts and 29 rows measure 10cm (4in) square over patt on 3mm (no. 11/US 2) needles
IT IS ESSENTIAL TO WORK TO THE STATED TENSION/GAUGE TO ACHIEVE SUCCESS

What you have to do:
Work back of purse in stocking/stockinette stitch and stripes. Work front of purse in honeycomb pattern and stripes. Knit flower decoration and twizzles separately. Sew zip fastener into purse opening. Construct flower and sew to purse. Add tassel decorations.

Instructions

PURSE:
With 3mm (no. 11/US 2) needles and A, cast on 31 sts. P 1 row (RS). Beg with a p row, cont in st st and stripe sequence of 2 rows each D, B, C and A.
Rep last 8 rows twice more, then work 2 rows each D, B and C and 1 row A, ending on WS.
Cont in honeycomb patt as foll:
1st row: (RS) With A, k to end.
2nd row: As 1st row.
3rd–6th rows: With B, work 4 rows in st st.
7th row: With A, k3, *sl next st off left needle and drop 4 rows down, insert point of right needle under strands and into st on 5th row down, insert left needle under strands and k st in usual way, catching strands in at same time – called k1b, k3, rep from * to end.
8th row: With A, k to end.
9th–12th rows: With C, work 4 rows in st st.
13th row: With A, k1, *k1b, k3, rep from * to last 2 sts, k1b, k1.
14th row: With A, k to end.
15th–18th rows: With D, work 4 rows in st st.
19th and 20th rows: As 7th and 8th rows.
21st–24th rows: With B, work 4 rows in st st.
25th and 26th rows: As 13th and 14th rows.
27th–30th rows: With C, work 4 rows in st st.
31st and 32nd rows: As 7th and 8th rows.
33rd–36th rows: With D, work 4 rows in st st.
37th and 38th rows: As 13th and 14th rows.
39th–42nd rows: With B, work 4 rows in st st.
43rd–44th rows: As 7th and 8th rows.

Abbreviations:

beg = beginning;
cm = centimetre(s);
cont = continue;
foll = follows;
k = knit; **p** = purl;
patt = pattern;
rep = repeat;
RS = right side;
sl = slip; **st(s)** = stitch(es);
st st = stocking/stockinette stitch;
tog = together;
WS = wrong side;
yfwd = yarn forward/yarn over to make a stitch

45th and 46th rows: With A, p 2 rows.
47th row: With A, k to end.
Cast/bind off knitwise.

TRUMPET FLOWER:

With 4mm (no. 8/US 6) needles and C, cast on 14 sts. P 1 row. Join in A. Beg with a k row, work 6 rows in st st.
Next row: K1, *yfwd, k2tog, rep from * to last st, k1.
Change to 3mm (no. 11/US 2) needles. Beg with a p row, work 9 rows in st st, ending with a WS row.
Unravel cast-on edge and put sts on to a spare needle with point facing in same direction as main needle. Holding two needles parallel and using a 4mm (no. 8/US 6) needle, k one st from each needle tog across row.
P 1 row. Cut off yarn leaving a long end. Thread cut end through rem sts, draw up and fasten off securely. Join side seam using mattress st.

TWIZZLES FOR ZIP AND FLOWER: (Make 3 in B and 2 in D)

With 4mm (no. 8/US 6) needles cast on 14 sts. Cast/bind off knitwise.
Make another one in A with 18 sts.

LEAF:

With 3mm (no. 11/US 2) needles and B, cast on 12 sts.
Next 2 rows: P12, turn, sl 1, k8, turn.
Next 2 rows: Sl 1, p6, turn, sl 1, k4, turn.
Next 2 rows: Sl 1, p3, turn, sl 1, k to end.

Next row: (RS) P to end.
Next 2 rows: K7, turn, p3, turn.
Next 2 rows: K4, turn, p5, turn.
Next 2 rows: K6, turn, p7, turn.
Next 2 rows: K8, turn, p to end.
Cast/bind off.

 # Making up

Sew in all ends. Block purse and press carefully. With RS
facing, fold purse in half and join side seams. Turn RS out
and sew zip fastener into opening, backstitching in place
with red sewing cotton.

Sew twizzle in A to zipper and attach a tassel made from
4 strands of D. Using crochet hook, attach tassels with 5
strands of D at each lower corner. Sew twizzles in D into
centre of trumpet flower. Using picture as a guide, sew on
leaf and twizzles in B, then attach flower to front of purse.

Child's sailor sweater

Perfect for playing on the beach, this hard-wearing sweater has a nautical look that is ideal for both boys and girls.

This easy drop-shoulder sweater is knitted in stocking/stockinette stitch with regular broken stripes in a contrast colour. It is a relaxed fit – perfect for a child – and it is a cool look, too!

The Yarn

Patons Diploma Gold DK is a mixture of 55% wool, 25% acrylic and 20% nylon that has the good looks of wool, yet is practical and hard-wearing, especially for children. It even looks good after machine washing.

There is a comprehensive colour range making plenty of choice for stripe combinations.

GETTING STARTED

 So easy to knit, with a minimum of shaping, that even a beginner could have a go

Size:

To fit chest: *61[66:71]cm/23[26:28]in*

Actual size: *74[80:85]cm/29[31½:33½]in*

Length: *39[43:47]cm/15½[17:18½]in*

Sleeve seam: *27[31:35]cm/10½[12:13¾]in*

Note: *Figures in square brackets [ ] refer to larger sizes; where there is only one set of figures, it applies to all sizes*

How much yarn:

4[5:6] x 50g (2oz) balls of Patons Diploma Gold DK, approx 120m (131 yards) per ball, in main colour M 1[1:2] balls in contrast colour C

Needles:

Pair of 3.75mm (no. 9/US 5) knitting needles
Pair of 4mm (no. 8/US 6) knitting needles
3.75mm (no. 9/US 5) circular knitting needle, 40cm (16in) long (for neckband)

Additional items:

3 stitch holders

Tension/gauge:

22 sts and 30 rows measure 10cm (4in) square over stripe patt on 4mm (no. 8/US 6) needles
IT IS ESSENTIAL TO WORK TO THE STATED TENSION/ GAUGE TO ACHIEVE SUCCESS

What you have to do:

Work in stocking/stockinette stitch (st st). Join in contrast-coloured yarn and make stripe by purling two rows. Leave shoulder stitches on stitch holders. Work simple shaping for front neck. Cast/bind off shoulder stitches together for invisible seam. Use circular needle to pick up stitches around neckline for neckband. Work neckband in rounds of stocking/stockinette stitch.

Instructions

Abbreviations:

beg = beginning; **cm** = centimetre(s);
cont = continue; **dec** = decrease(ing);
foll = following; **inc** = increase(ing);
k = knit; **p** = purl; **patt** = pattern;
rem = remaining; **rep** = repeat;
RS = right side; **sl** = slip; **st(s)** = stitch(es);
st st = stocking/stockinette stitch;
tog = together; **WS** = wrong side

BACK:

With 3.75mm (no. 9/US 5) needles and M, cast
on 82[88:94] sts. Beg with a k row, work 10
rows in st st.
Change to 4mm (no. 8/US 6) needles. Cont in
stripe patt as foll:
1st row: (RS) With C, p to end.
2nd row: With C, p to end.
3rd–12th rows: With M and beg with a k row,
work 10 rows in st st.
These 12 rows form patt.* Rep them 8[9:10]
times more.
Next row: (RS) With C, p26[28:30], cut off C,
sl next 30[32:34] sts on to a st holder and leave
for neckband, rejoin C to next st and p to end.
Sl both sets of shoulder sts on to two more
st holders.

FRONT:
Work as given for Back to *. Rep them 7[8:9] times more.
Shape neck:
Next row: (RS) With C, p33[35:37] sts, turn and leave rem sts on a spare needle.
** Cont in patt, dec 1 st at neck edge on next 7 rows. 26[28:30] sts. Work 5 rows straight, ending with 1st p row in C. Do not cut off C.**
Shape shoulder:
Return to back sts: with WS facing and beg at outside left shoulder edge, sl 26[28:30] sts from left shoulder on to spare needle.
With RS of both shoulder pieces tog, using C and holding both needles with shoulder sts in left hand – front sts in front of back sts – and points of needles tog, cast/bind off loosely knitwise both pieces tog, taking 1 st from front tog with 1 st from back each time.
Sl centre front 16[18:20] sts on to a st holder, rejoin C to rem 33[35:37] sts and p to end. Work as given for left side of Front from ** to **.

Shape shoulder:
Return to Back sts: with WS facing and beg at inside right neck edge, sl 26[28:30] sts from right shoulder on to a spare needle.
Work as given for left shoulder from *** to ***.

SLEEVES: (Make 2)
With 3.75mm (no. 9/US 5) needles and M, cast on 50[54:58] sts. Beg with a k row, work 10 rows in st st. Change to 4mm (no. 8/US 6) needles. Cont in stripe patt as given for Back, inc 1 st at each end of next and every foll 6th row to 74[82:90] sts. Work 5 rows straight, ending with 10th row in M. Cast/bind off.

NECKBAND:
With 3.75mm (no. 9/US 5) circular needle, M and RS of work facing, pick up and k 12 sts down left front neck, k across 16[18:20] centre front neck sts from holder, pick up and k 12 sts up right front neck and k across 30[32:34] centre back neck sts from holder. 70[74:78] sts. Work 10[12:14] rounds in st st (every round k). Cast/bind off fairly loosely.

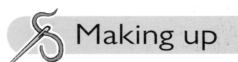

Making up

Press according to directions on ball band.
Sew in sleeves approximately 17[18.5:20]cm/6¾[7¼:8]in down from shoulders. Join side and sleeve seams.

Fun family slippers

Slippers in every size for all the family – this has to be the ultimate hand-made gift.

From baby to grandma, these slippers are for all the family. Worked in cotton yarn, with ribbed soles and heel and moss/seed stitch uppers, they are decorated with crochet trims and pompoms in contrasting colours.

The Yarn

Debbie Bliss Cotton DK is 100% pure cotton in a soft but sturdy finish that is ideal for these accessories. If you want to mix and match toning shades as we have done for our slippers, there are plenty of colours to choose from.

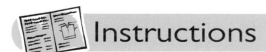 Instructions

Abbreviations:
beg = beginning; **ch** = chain; **cm** = centimetre(s); **cont** = continue; **dc** = double crochet; **dec** = decrease(ing); **foll** = following; **k** – knit; **p** = purl; **patt** = pattern; **rem** = remain; **rep** = repeat; **RS** = right side; **ss** = slipstitch; **st(s)** = stitch(es); **tog** = together; **WS** = wrong side

GETTING STARTED

 Easy to make in basic stitches with simple shaping

Size:
To fit foot length: 10[14:18:20:22]cm/4[5½:7:8:8½]in
Note: Figures in square brackets [ ] refer to larger sizes; where there is only one set of figures, it applies to all sizes

How much yarn:
1[1:2:2:3] x 50g (2oz) balls of Debbie Bliss Cotton DK, approx 84m (92 yards) per ball
Oddments of yarn in contrast colours for decorations

Needles:
Pair of 4mm (no. 8/US 6) knitting needles

Additional items:
2 small buttons for baby's slippers
4mm (no. 8/US 6) crochet hook for baby's and adult's slippers

Tension/gauge:
22 sts and 30 rows to 10cm (4in) square over moss/seed st on 4mm (no. 8/US 6) needles
IT IS ESSENTIAL TO WORK TO THE STATED TENSION /GAUGE TO ACHIEVE SUCCESS

What you have to do:
Work in single (k1, p1) rib. Work in moss/seed stitch. Simple shaping by working two or three stitches together. Keep moss/seed stitch and rib patterns correct over shaping. Decorate with simple crochet edging, flower motifs or pompoms (optional).

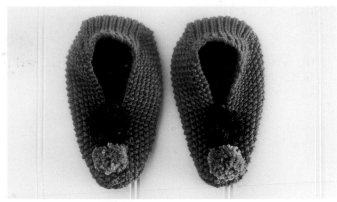

Note: Examples shown are 1st (baby's), 3rd (child's) and 5th (adult's) sizes. To increase, or reduce, foot size, find the size that is closest to your foot length and work more, or fewer, rows straight before ** in pattern to achieve required length.

SLIPPERS:

With 4mm (no. 8/US 6) needles cast on 11[15:19:19:21] sts and beg at back of heel.

1st row: (RS) P1, *k1, p1, rep from * to end.
2nd row: K1, *p1, k1, rep from * to end.
Rep these 2 rows to form single rib 3[5:7:8:8] times more.

Shape sides:

Next row: (RS) Cast on 8[12:14:16:18] sts, (p1, k1) 4[6:7:8:9] times over these sts, rib to end as set.
Next row: Cast on 8[12:14:16:18] sts, (k1, p1) 4[6:7:8:9] times over these sts, rib next 11[15:19:19:21] sts as set, (k1, p1) 4[6:7:8:9] times. 27[39:47:51:57] sts.
Next row: (RS) (P1, k1) 4[6:7:8:9] times, rib 11[15:19:19:21] as set, (p1, k1) 4[6:7:8:9] times.
Next row: (K1, p1) 4[6:7:8:9] times, rib 11[15:19:19:21] as set, (k1, p1) 4[6:7:8:9] times. Rep last 2 rows until work measures 4[6:8:8:9]cm/1½[2½:3:3:3½]in from second cast-on row. ** (Adjust foot length here if required.)

Shape foot:

Next row: Patt 7[11:13:15:17], p2tog, rib 9[13:17:17:19], p2tog, patt to end. Work 3 rows in patt. Insert markers at each end of last row.
Next row: Patt 6[10:12:14:16], p2tog, rib 9[13:17:17:19], p2tog, patt to end.

2nd, 3rd, 4th and 5th sizes only:

Cont to dec as set on foll 4th rows [1:2:2:4] times.

All sizes:

23[33:39:43:45] sts. Patt 1 row. Now dec at either side of central rib as set on every RS row until 19[23:29:31:35] sts rem. Patt 1 row.

1st and 2nd sizes only:

Next row: Patt 3, p2tog, rib 0[2], k3tog, rib 3, k3tog, rib 0[2], p2tog, patt to end. Patt 1 row.
Next row: Patt 2, p2tog, rib 1[3], p3tog, rib 1[3], p2tog, patt to end. 9[13] sts.
Patt 1 row. Cut off yarn, thread through rem sts, pull up tightly and secure.

3rd, 4th and 5th sizes only:

Next row: Patt 4[5:6], p2tog, rib 4, k3tog, rib 3[3:5], k3tog, rib 4, p2tog, patt to end. Patt 1 row.
Next row: Patt 3[4:5], p2tog, rib 2, k3tog, rib 3[3:5], k3tog, rib 2, p2tog, patt to end. Patt 1 row.
Next row: Patt 2[3:4], p2tog, rib 3[3:4], p3tog[p3tog:k3tog], rib 3[3:4], p2tog, patt to end. Patt 1 row. Cut off yarn, thread through rem sts, pull up tightly and secure.

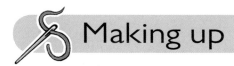 Making up

Join back heel seams with backstitch.

Decorations:

Baby's slippers: With 4mm (no. 8/US 6) crochet hook, contrast yarn and RS facing, work a row of double

HOW TO
CROCHET A FLOWER

This makes the large flower, which is attached to the adult slippers, and the instructions are amended to form the smaller flower.

1 Make a slip knot on the crochet hook and then make 6 chains by passing the hook over and under the yarn, catching the yarn and bringing it through the loop on the hook.

2 Join the chain into a ring by making a slip stitch into the first chain. To do this, insert the hook into the chain, catch the yarn and draw it back through the chain and the loop on the hook.

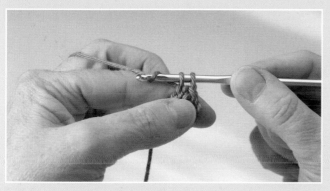

3 Make a double (US single) crochet stitch, working into the centre of the ring and then make 10 chains.

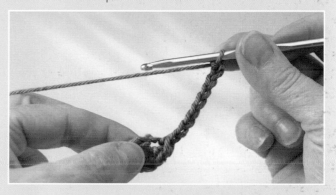

4 Repeat this seven times more to make the 'petals' of the flower and then join with a slip stitch to the first double (US single) crochet and fasten off.

(US single) crochet around entire front edge of each slipper. Join centre front seam (by overcasting on WS or work) below markers. Sew a small button onto each slipper.

Child's slippers: Join centre front seam (by overcasting on WS of work) below markers. Make two pompoms 2cm (¾in) in diameter from 1st contrast colour and two pompoms 1cm (½in) in diameter from 2nd contrast colour. Sew two pompoms (one in each size and colour) to centre front seam as shown.

Adult's slippers: Join centre front seam (by overcasting on WS of work). Make two large flowers in 1st contrast colour and four small flowers in 2nd contrast colour as follows:

Large flower: With 4mm (no. 8/US 6) crochet hook make 6ch. Join with a ss into 1st ch to form a ring**, (1dc/US sc into ring, 10ch) 8 times, join with a ss to 1st dc/US sc. Fasten off.

Small flower: As Large flower to **, (1dc/US sc into ring, 5ch) 6 times, join with a ss to 1st dc/US sc. Fasten off. Sew large flower to front of slipper and two smaller flowers on sides as shown.

Ladybird hat

Get your toddler in touch with nature with this cute ladybird hat.

No toddler will mind wearing this hat. Worked in sections of stocking/ stockinette stitch with big black spots, it even has authentic-looking antennae.

GETTING STARTED

 Although fabric is easy stocking/ stockinette stitch, working spots from chart will need some concentration

Size:
To fit head circumference approximately 48cm (19in)

How much yarn:
1 x 50g (2oz) ball of Debbie Bliss Baby Cashmerino, approx 125m (137 yards) per ball, in each of two colours A and B

Needles:
Pair of 3.25mm (no. 10/US 3) knitting needles
Set of 2mm (no. 14/US 0) double-pointed knitting needles

Tension/gauge:
25 sts and 34 rows measure 10cm (4in) square over st st on 3.25mm (no. 10/US 3) needles
IT IS ESSENTIAL TO WORK TO THE STATED TENSION/GAUGE TO ACHIEVE SUCCESS

What you have to do:
Work in stocking/stockinette stitch. Work spots from chart, using intarsia technique and stranding yarn not in use across back of work. Shape crown with simple paired decreases. Work cord for antennae on double-pointed knitting needles.

The Yarn
Debbie Bliss Baby Cashmerino is a blend of 55% merino wool with 33% microfibre and 12% cashmere making it warm, soft and luxurious for a small child, yet practical as well. There is a striking colour palette to choose from containing a lot more interesting colours than the usual baby shades.

 ## Instructions

HAT:
With 3.25mm (no. 10/US 3) needles and A, cast on 120 sts. Beg with a k row, work 12 rows in st st for roll edge, then work a further 10 rows. Cont in st st, placing spot patt from chart and stranding colour not in use loosely across back of work as foll:

1st row: (RS) K across 20 sts of 1st row of chart, k20 A, (k across 20 sts of 1st row of chart) twice, k20 A, k across 20 sts of 1st row of chart.

Cont in st st and patt as set from chart until 18 rows have been completed.

Abbreviations:

alt = alternate;
beg = beginning;
cm = centimetre(s);
cont = continue;
dec = decrease;
foll = follow(s)(ing);
k = knit; **p** = purl;
patt = pattern;
psso = pass slipped
stitch over;
rem = remaining;
RS = right side; **sl** = slip;
st(s) = stitch(es);
st st = stocking/stockinette
stitch;
tog = together

Next row: (RS) K20 A, k across 20 sts of
1st row of chart, k40 A, k across 20 sts of
1st row of chart, k20 A.
Cont in st st and patt as set from chart until
18 rows have been completed. Cut off B
and cont in A only.

Shape crown:

1st row: (Sl 1, k1, psso, k16, k2tog)
6 times.
2nd and foll alt rows: P to end.
3rd row: (Sl 1, k1, psso, k14, k2tog)
6 times.
5th row: (Sl 1, k1, psso, k12, k2tog)
6 times.
Cont to dec 12 sts in this way on foll alt
rows until 24 sts rem, ending with a p row.
Next row: (K2tog) to end. 12 sts.
Next row: (P2tog) to end. 6 sts.
Cut off yarn, thread through rem sts, draw
up and fasten off securely.

ANTENNAE: (Make 2)
With 2mm (no. 14/US 0) double-pointed
needles and B, cast on 5 sts. Work knitted
cord as foll:
1st row: K to end.
2nd row: Do not turn. Slide sts back to
beg of needle, pull yarn firmly and k to end.
Rep 2nd row until cord measures 14cm
(5½in) long. Cast/bind off.

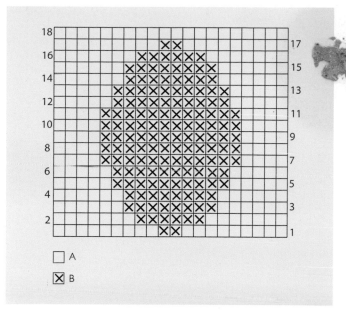

Making up

Do not press or flatten roll edge. Join back seam with mattress stitch. Roll top 4cm (1½in) of cord to RS and secure then stitch opposite end to top of hat as shown. With B, work backstitch up centre front and down centre back of hat, working on top of seam.

Patchwork baby blanket

Make this delightful blanket with its simple but effective design for a lucky baby, or enlarge it to fit a child's bed.

Cover a crib or pushchair with this soft and colourful patchwork blanket. Easy to knit in squares of striped stocking/stockinette stitch and plain moss/seed stitch, it makes the perfect present for a new baby.

GETTING STARTED

 Squares are easy to knit in basic stitches but neatness and care is required in sewing in ends and making up into patchwork

Size:
Blanket measures 55cm x 70cm (21½in x 27½in)

How much yarn:
Debbie Bliss Baby Cashmerino, approx 125m (137 yards) per ball, 3 x 50g (2oz) balls in main colour A
1 ball in each of six contrast colours B, C, D, E, F and G

Needles:
Pair of 5mm (no. 6/US 8) knitting needles

Tension/gauge:
With yarn used DOUBLE, 19 sts and 26 rows measure 10cm (4in) square over st st and 18 sts and 30 rows measure 10cm (4in) square over moss/seed st on 5mm (no. 6/US 8) needles
IT IS ESSENTIAL TO WORK TO THE STATED TENSION/GAUGE TO ACHIEVE SUCCESS

What you have to do:
Knit with two strands of yarn (double). Work in stocking/stockinette stitch. Knit stripes, joining in and cutting off colours as required. Work in moss/seed stitch. Sew in yarn ends from stripes. Join squares together, following diagram, to form patchwork. Pick up stitches around edges for borders and work in garter stitch.

The Yarn
Debbie Bliss Baby Cashmerino is a luxuriously soft yarn, containing 55% merino wool, 33% microfibre and 12% cashmere, that is equivalent to 4-ply (fingering) in weight. The shade range is contemporary and comprehensive, making it ideal for colourwork projects and completed items can be machine washed at 30° (86°F).

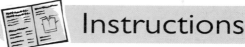 ## Instructions

STRIPED PATT:
1st–3rd rows: Work in A.
4th–6th rows: Work in B.
7th–9th rows: Work in A.
10th–12th rows: Work in C.
13th–15th rows: Work in A.
16th–18th rows: Work in D.
19th–21st rows: Work in A.
22nd–24th rows: Work in E.
25th–27th rows: Work in A.
28th–30th rows: Work in F.
31st–33rd rows: Work in A.
34th–36th rows: Work in G.
37th–39th rows: Work in A.

BLANKET:
Striped square 1: (Make 2)
With A USED DOUBLE, cast on 29 sts. Beg with a k row, cont in st st and work 39 rows of stripe patt, joining in and cutting off colours as required. Cast/bind off pwise on WS of work.

Striped square 2:
With A USED DOUBLE, cast on 29 sts. Beg with a k row, cont in st st and work in striped patt as foll: work

Abbreviations:

beg = beginning;
cm = centimetre(s);
cont = continue; **k** = knit;
kwise = knitwise; **p** = purl;
m1 = make a stitch by picking up horizontal loop lying between needles and working into back of it;
patt = pattern;
pwise = purlwise;
rep = repeat;
RS = right side;
st(s) = stitch(es);
st st = stocking/stockinette stitch;
WS = wrong side

25th–39th rows, then 4th–27th rows. Cast/bind off pwise on WS of work.

Striped square 3: With A USED DOUBLE, cast on 29 sts. Beg with a k row, cont in st st and work in striped patt as foll: work 19th–39th rows, then 4th–21st rows. Cast/bind off pwise on WS of work.

Striped square 4: With 5mm (no. 6/US 8) needles and A USED DOUBLE, cast on 29 sts. Beg with a k row, cont in st st and work in striped patt as foll: work 31st–39th rows, then 4th–33rd rows. Cast off pwise on WS of work.

Striped square 5: With A USED DOUBLE, cast on 29 sts. Beg with a k row, cont in st st and work in striped patt as foll: work 13th–39th rows, then 4th–15th rows. Cast/bind off pwise on WS of work.

Moss/seed stitch square: (Make 6)
With B USED DOUBLE, cast on 27 sts.
1st row: (RS) K1, *p1, k1, rep from * to end.
Rep last row to form patt until square measures 15cm (6in), ending with a WS row. Cast/bind off in moss/seed st. Make a further 5 moss/seed stitch squares, one in each of C, D, E, F and G.

Making up

Press squares carefully following instructions on ball band. Join together using backstitch and following the order as shown in the chart (right).

UPPER BORDER:

With D USED DOUBLE and RS of work facing, pick up and k78 sts along upper edge of Blanket.
**1st row: (WS) K to end.
2nd row: K1, m1, k to last st, m1, k1. 80 sts. Rep last 2 rows 7 times more, ending with a RS row. 94 sts.
Cast/bind off kwise (on WS).**

LOWER BORDER:

With D USED DOUBLE and RS of work facing, pick up and k78 sts along lower edge of Blanket. Work as given for Upper border from ** to **.

SIDE BORDERS: (Alike)

With 5mm (no. 6/US 8) needles, D USED DOUBLE and RS of work facing, pick up and k104 sts along side edge of Blanket.
**1st row: (WS) K to end.
2nd row: K1, m1, k to last st, m1, k1. 106 sts. Rep last 2 rows 7 times more, ending with a RS row. 120 sts.
Cast/bind off kwise (on WS).**
Join shaped row-ends of Borders.

Striped square 1	Moss/seed stitch square in B	Striped square 2
Moss/seed stitch square in G	Striped square 3	Moss/seed stitch square in C
Striped square 4	Moss/seed stitch square in D	Striped square 1
Moss/seed stitch square in E	Striped square 5	Moss/seed stitch square in F

Teddy steps out

Give your favourite teddy his own outfit. This smart hat, scarf and bag will make him stand out from the crowd!

Kit out teddy in a cheery, striped pompom hat and scarf and make him a bag to match. All the pieces are worked in basic stitches so even a child could have a go making them.

GETTING STARTED

 Each piece is easy to make in simple stripes

Size:

For a teddy approximately 25cm (10in) in height
Hat: *circumference approximately 33cm (13in)*
Scarf: *50cm long x 4.5cm wide (20in x 1¾in)*
Bag: *7cm (2¾in) square*

How much yarn:

1 x 50g ball of Patons Gold Diploma DK, approx 120m (131 yards) per ball, in each of five colours A, B, C, D and E

Needles:

Pair of 3.25mm (no. 10/US 3) knitting needles
Pair of 4mm (no. 8/US 6) knitting needles
Pair of 4mm (no. 8/US 6) double-pointed needles

Additional items:

1 press stud (popper snap), pompom kit or cardboard

Tension/gauge:

22 sts and 30 rows measure 10cm (4in) square over st st on 4mm (no. 8/US 6) needles
IT IS ESSENTIAL TO WORK TO THE STATED TENSION/GAUGE TO ACHIEVE SUCCESS

What you have to do:

For hat, work in reverse stocking/stockinette stitch with knit ribs. For scarf, work in garter stitch. For bag, work in stocking/stockinette stitch. For all pieces, work in stripes as directed, carrying colour not in use up side of work where possible. Make pompom trims. Make cord for bag on double-pointed needles.

The Yarn

Patons Diploma Gold DK is a mixture of 55% wool, 25% acrylic and 20% nylon. It is machine washable and there are plenty of colours to choose from for interesting stripe patterns.

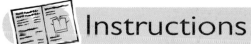 Instructions

HAT:

With 3.25mm (no. 10/US 3) needles and A, cast on 72 sts.
1st row: K1, (p1, k1) to last st, p1.
Rep last row 3 times more.
Change to 4mm (no. 8/US 6) needles. Join in B and working in stripe sequence of 2 rows B, 4 rows C, 2 rows A, 6 rows D and 2 rows E throughout, cont as foll:
Next row: (RS) K1, p10, (k2, p10) to last st, k1.
Next row: P1, k10, (p2, k10) to last st, p1.
Next row: K1, m1, p10, (m1, k2, m1, p10) to last st, m1, k1. 84 sts.
Next row: P1, k12, (p2, k12) to last st, p1.
Next row: K1, m1, p12, (m1, k2, m1, p12) to last st, m1, k1. 96 sts.
Next row: P1, k14, (p2, k14) to last st, p1.
Next row: K1, p14, (k2, p14) to last st, k1.
Next row: P1, k14, (p2, k14) to last st, p1.

Shape crown:

Keeping ribs on same sts as set, cont as foll:
Next row: K1, p6, p2tog, p6, (k2, p6, p2tog, p6) to last st, k1. 90 sts.

Abbreviations:

alt = alternate;
beg = beginning;
cm = centimetre(s);
cont = continue;
dec = decrease(ing);
foll = following;
g st = garter stitch (every row knit);
inc = increase(ing);
k = knit;
m I = make 1 stitch by picking up strand lying between needles and working into back of it;
p = purl;
rem = remain(ing);
rep = repeat;
RS = right side;
skpo = slip one, knit one, pass slipped stitch over;
st(s) = stitch(es);
st st = stocking/stockinette stitch;
tbl = through back of loop

Next row: P1, k13, (p2, k13) to last st, p1.
Next row: K1, p6, p2tog, p5, (k2, p6, p2tog, p5) to last st, k1. 84 sts.
Next row: P1, k12, (p2, k12) to last st, p1.
Next row: K1, p5, p2tog, p5, (k2, p5, p2tog, p5) to last st, k1. 78 sts.
Next row: P1, k11, (p2, k11) to last st, p1.
Work a further 14 rows, AT SAME TIME dec 6 sts in the same way on every alt row until 36 sts rem.
Next row: K1, (p2tog) twice, (k2, (p2tog) twice) to last st, k1. 24 sts.
Next row: P1, k2, (p2, k2) to last st, p1.
Next row: (K2tog) to end. 12 sts.
Next row: (P2tog) to end. 6 sts.
Cut off yarn, thread through rem sts, draw up tightly and fasten off.

SCARF:

(Knitted lengthwise)
With 4mm (no. 8/US 6) needles and A, cast on 110 sts.
Cont in g st, work 18 rows in stripe sequence as foll:

2 rows A, *2 rows B, 4 rows C, 2 rows A, 6 rows D and 2 rows E. * Cast/bind off.

BAG:
Main part:

With 4mm (no. 8/US 6) needles and A, cast on 18 sts.
K 2 rows. Join in B. Beg with a k row, cont in st st and rep 16 rows in same stripe sequence as Scarf from * to * until work measures 14cm (5½in) from beg, ending with a RS row.

Shape flap:

Next row: K3, p to last 3 sts, k3.
Next row: K to end.
Next row: K3, p to last 3 sts, k3.
Next row: K3, skpo, k to last 5 sts, k2tog, k3. Rep last 2 rows twice more. 12 sts.
Next row: K3, p to last 3 sts, k3.
K 2 more rows. Cast/bind off.

Strap:

With 4mm (no. 8/US 6) double-pointed needles and A, cast on 4 sts. K 1 row.
Next row: * Without turning work and RS facing, slide sts to other end of needle and, pulling yarn from left-hand side of sts to right across back, k1 tbl, k3. *
Rep from * to *, remembering to pull yarn tightly across back and always working a k row, until strap measures 30cm (12in).
Cast/bind off.

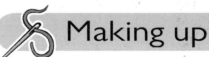 ## Making up

HAT:

Sew in all ends. Using mattress stitch, sew row ends together, starting at the crown, to form centre back seam. Make a pompom approximately 3.5cm (1¼in) in diameter using B and sew it to centre of crown.

SCARF:

Sew in all ends. Gather each end of the scarf. Make two pompoms approximately 3.5cm (1¼in) in diameter using B and sew one to each gathered end of scarf.

BAG:

Sew in all ends. Fold bag so that cast-on edge is just below beg of flap. With RS facing, sew side seams, curving seam slightly towards bottom edge of bag. Sew each end of strap inside top edge of bag at side seams. Sew press stud (popper snap) to underside of flap and front of bag.

Lace-edged blanket

Create this soft blanket for a new arrival – it makes a wonderful gift that is both beautiful and practical.

Forget the hassle of sewing squares together, this textured blanket in a chunky yarn is worked in one piece and then the lace edging, in a finer weight yarn, is sewn on afterwards.

GETTING STARTED

The pattern is easy to follow but working a large piece of fabric can be quite demanding

Size:
Blanket is 116cm x 140cm (45½cm x 55in), including edging

How much yarn:
15 x 50g (2oz) balls of Sirdar Click Chunky, approx 75m (82 yards) per ball
2 x 100g (3½oz) balls of Sirdar Supersoft Aran, approx 236m (258 yards) per ball

Needles:
Pair of 5.5mm (no. 5/US 9) knitting needles
6.5mm (no. 3/US 10½) circular knitting needle, 100cm (40in) long

Tension/gauge:
14 sts and 19 rows measure 10cm (4 in) square over reverse st st in Denim Chunky on 6.5mm (no. 3/US 10½) needles
IT IS ESSENTIAL TO WORK TO THE STATED TENSION/GAUGE TO ACHIEVE SUCCESS

What you have to do:
Use circular needle for large number of stitches and work in rows. Work in stocking/stockinette stitch and reverse stocking/stockinette block pattern, making lace 'flower' in centre of reverse stocking/stockinette stitch squares. Make strip of lace-patterned edging where extra stitches are made and lost over several rows. Sew edging around blanket.

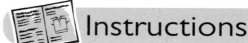
Instructions

BLANKET:
With 6.5mm (no. 3/US 10½) circular needle and Click Chunky, cast on 143 sts. Working forwards and backwards in rows, cont in patt as foll:
1st row: (RS) K13, *p13, k13, rep from * to end.
2nd row: P13, *k13, p13, rep from * to end.
3rd–4th rows: As 1st and 2nd.
5th row: As 1st.
6th row: P13, *k4, sl 1, k1, psso, yfwd, k1, yfwd, k2tog, k4, p13, rep from * to end.
7th row: As 1st.
8th row: P13, *k3, sl 1, k1, psso, yfwd, k3, yfwd, k2tog, k3, p13, rep from * to end.
9th row: K13, *p6, make bobble (mb) as foll: (k1, p1, k1) all into next st, turn and p3, turn and k3, turn and p3, turn and sl 1, k2tog, psso, p6, k13, rep from * to end.
10th row: P13, *k3, k2tog, yfwd, k3, yfwd, sl 1, k1, psso,

The Yarn
Sirdar Click Chunky contain 70% acrylic and 30% wool and Sirdar Supersoft Aran is 100% acrylic. The chunky weight knits up quickly but it is light and soft at the same time. Both yarns come in a wide range of colours – we chose Click Chunky in Lamb (142) and Supersoft Aran in Oatmeal (859)

Abbreviations:

alt = alternate;
cm = centimetre(s);
cont = continue;
foll = follow(s)(ing);
k = knit; **p** = purl;
patt = pattern;
psso = pass slipped
stitch over;
rep = repeat;
RS = right side; **sl** = slip;
st(s) = stitch(es);
tog = together;
yfwd = yarn forward/yarn
over to make one stitch

k3, p13, rep from * to end.

11th row: As 1st.

12th row: P13, *k4, k2tog, yfwd, k1, yfwd, sl 1, k1, psso, k4, p13, rep from * to end.

13th-16th rows: Rep 1st and 2nd rows twice.

17th row: P13, *k13, p13, rep from * to end.

18th row: K13, *p13, k13, rep from * to end.

19th–20th rows: As 17th and 18th.

21st row: As 17th.

22nd row: K4, sl 1, k1, psso, yfwd, k1, yfwd, k2tog, k4, *p13, k4, sl 1, k1, psso, yfwd, k1, yfwd, k2tog, k4 rep from * to end.

23rd row: As 17th.

24th row: K3, sl 1, k1, psso, yfwd, k3, yfwd, k2tog, k3, *p13, k3, sl 1, k1, psso, yfwd, k3, yfwd, k2tog, k3, rep from * to end.

25th row: P6, mb, p6, *k13, p6, mb, p6, rep from * to end.

26th row: K3, k2tog, yfwd, k3, yfwd, sl 1, k1, psso, k3, *p13, k3, k2tog, yfwd, k3, yfwd, sl 1, k1, psso, k3, rep from * to end.

27th row: As 17th.

28th row: K4, k2tog, yfwd, k1, yfwd, sl 1, k1, psso, k4, *p13, k4, k2tog, yfwd, k1, yfwd, sl 1, k1, psso, k4, rep from * to end.

29th–32nd rows: Rep 17th and 18th rows twice.

These 32 rows form patt. Rep them 6 times more, then work 1st–16th rows again. Cast/bind off.

LACE EDGING:

With 5.5mm (no. 5/US 9) needles and Supersift Aran, cast on 9 sts.

1st and foll alt rows: K to end.

2nd row: K3, k2tog, yfwd, k2tog, (yfwd, k1) twice.

4th row: K2, (k2tog, yfwd) twice, k3, yfwd, k1.

6th row: K1, (k2tog, yfwd) twice, k5, yfwd, k1.

8th row: K3, (yfwd, k2tog) twice, k1, k2tog, yfwd, k2tog.

10th row: K4, yfwd, k2tog, yfwd, k3tog, yfwd, k2tog.

12th row: K5, yfwd, k3tog, yfwd, k2tog. Rep these 12 rows until edging measures about 468cm, ending with a 12th patt row. Cast/bind off.

HOW TO
USE CIRCULAR NEEDLES

A circular needle is normally used to make a tubular piece of knitting, as you knit round in a continuous circle, but they can be used to work in rows where there are a lot of stitches. Circular needles consist of two straight needles joined by a flexible plastic wire. They are available in different sizes just like ordinary knitting needles and also come in several lengths.

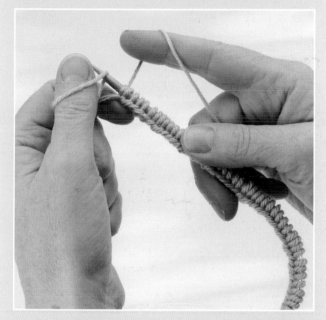

Making up

Pin lace edging in position butted up around outer edge of blanket, gathering it slightly to ease around corners. Slip stitch in place, oversewing ends of edging together. Lightly steam outer edges of edging so that it lies flat.

Cast on the stitches as you would for ordinary knitting using a regular needle. Now transfer the needle point with the last cast-on stitches to your left hand. Knit the first row in the usual way, moving the stitches up the wire onto the rigid needle point to be worked. At the end of the first row repeat the process, changing the needle point with the last stitches worked to your left hand.

Party cardigan

Sparkle at your party with this fabulous top decorated with crystal beads and sequins.

The perfect cover-up for a young lady on her way to a party, this knotted-style cardigan in a luxurious angora-blend yarn is embellished with gorgeous beads and sequins.

GETTING STARTED

 Fairly easy design but pay attention to working front band and ties for a neat finish

Size:

To fit chest: *51[56:66:71]cm/20[22:26:28]in*
Actual size: *60[65:71:76]cm/23½[25½:28:30]in*
Length: *27.5[30.5:34:36]cm/10¾[12:13¼:14]in*
Sleeve seam: *25[27:29:31]cm/10[10½:11½:12¼]in*
Note: *Figures in square brackets [ ] refer to larger sizes; where there is only one set of figures, it applies to all sizes*

How much yarn:

2[2:3:3] x 50g (2oz) balls of Orkney Angora 'St Magnus' 50/50 DK, approx 200m (219 yards) per ball

Needles:

Pair of 3.75mm (no. 9/US 5) knitting needles
Pair of 4.5mm (no. 7/US 7) knitting needles
3.75mm (no. 9/US 5) circular knitting needle

Additional items:

Stitch holder, 150cm (60in) silver sequin trim
Silver beads and sequins for decoration
Sewing needle and matching thread

Tension/gauge:

22 sts and 28 rows measure 10cm (4in) square over st st using 4.5mm (no. 7/US 7) needles
IT IS ESSENTIAL TO WORK TO THE STATED TENSION/GAUGE TO ACHIEVE SUCCESS

What you have to do:

Work lower edges in garter stitch (knit every row) and main fabric in stocking/stockinette stitch. Use simple shaping for armholes and front edges. Use a circular needle to pick up large number of stitches in front bands and ties. Sew on sequin trim and beads.

The Yarn

Orkney Angora 'St Magnus' 50/50 DK is a luxurious blend of finest grade angora with best-quality lambswool. Dyed in thirty five shades, this yarn has a fabulous lustre that enhances its natural beauty for designer knitwear.

Instructions

Abbreviations:

alt = alternate;
beg = beginning;
cm = centimetre(s);
cont = continue;
dec = decrease;
foll = following;
inc = increase(ing);
k = knit; **p** = purl;
psso = pass slipped stitch
over; **rem** = remaining;
rep = repeat;
RS = right side; **sl** = slip;
st(s) = stitch(es);
st st = stocking/stockinette
stitch;
tog = together;
WS = wrong side

BACK:

With 3.75mm (no. 9/US 5) needles cast on 66[72:78:84] sts. K 2 rows. Change to 4.5mm (no. 7/US 7) needles. Beg with a k row, work 42[46:50:54] rows in st st, ending with a p row.

Shape armholes:

Cast/bind off 3[3:4:4] sts at beg of next 2 rows. Dec 1 st at each end of next and 4[5:5:6] foll alt rows. 50[54:58:62] sts. Work 19[21:25:27] rows straight, ending with a p row.

Shape back neck and shoulders:

Next row: (RS) K13[14:15:16], turn and complete this side of neck first. Dec 1 st at neck edge on next 3 rows. Cast/bind off rem 10[11:12:13] sts. With RS of work facing, sl centre 24[26:28:30] sts on to a holder for back neck, rejoin yarn to next st and k to end. Dec 1 st at neck edge on next 3 rows. Cast/bind off rem 10[11:12:13] sts.

LEFT FRONT:

With 3.75mm (no. 9/US 5) needles cast on 37[41:45:49] sts. K 2 rows. Change to 4.5mm (no. 7/US 7) needles.

Shape front edge:

Next row: (RS) K to last 3 sts, k2tog, k1.
Beg with a p row, work 3 rows in st st. Rep last 4 rows 9[10:11:12] times more, then work dec row again. 26[29:32:35] sts. P 1 row, ending at armhole edge.

Shape armhole:

Next row: (RS) Cast/bind off 3[3:4:4] sts, k to end.

P 1 row.
Next row: K2tog, k to last 3 sts, k2tog, k1. P 1 row.
Next row: K2tog, k to end. P 1 row.
* Cont as set, dec 1 st at front edge on next and foll 4th rows, AT SAME TIME dec 1 st at armhole edge on next and foll alt rows until 15[17:19:20] sts rem. Keeping armhole edge straight, cont to dec at front edge only as before until 10[11:12:13] sts rem.
Work 3 rows straight. Cast/bind off.

RIGHT FRONT:

With 3.75mm (no. 9/US 5) needles cast on 37[41:45:49] sts. K 2 rows. Change to 4.5mm (no. 7/US 7) needles.

Shape front edge:

Next row: (RS) K1, sl 1, k1, psso, k to end.
Beg with a p row, work 3 rows in st st. Rep last 4 rows 9[10:11:12] times more, then work dec row again. 26[29:32:35] sts. P 1 and k 1 row, ending at armhole edge.

Shape armhole:

Next row: (WS) Cast/bind off 3[3:4:4] sts, p to end.
Next row: (RS) K1, sl 1, k1, psso, k to last 2 sts, sl 1, k1, psso. P 1 row.
Next row: K to last 2 sts, sl 1, k1, psso.
P 1 row. Now complete as given for Left front from * to end.

SLEEVES: (Make 2)

With 3.75mm (no. 9/US 5) needles cast on 40[42:44:46] sts. K 2 rows.

Change to 4.5mm (no. 7/US 7) needles. Beg with a k row, work 18 rows in st st, ending with a p row. Inc 1 st at each end of next and every foll 6th row to 56[60:66:70] sts. Work 7[7:1:1] rows straight, ending with a p row.

Shape top:

Cast/bind off 3[3:4:4] st at beg of next 2 rows. Dec 1 st at each end of next 8 rows. 34[38:42:46] sts. Cast/bind off 7[8:9:10] sts at beg of next 2 rows. Cast/bind off rem 20[22:24:26] sts.

FRONT BAND AND TIES:

Join shoulder seams.

With 3.75mm (no. 9/US 5) circular needle cast on 30[30:32:32] sts for first tie, then with RS of work facing, pick up and k60[66:72:78] sts up right front edge to shoulder, 3 sts down right back neck, k across 24[26:28:30] back neck sts on holder, pick up and k 3 sts up left back neck, 60[66:72:78] sts down left front edge, then cast on 30[30:32:32] sts for second tie. 210[224:242:256] sts. Working forwards and backwards in rows, k 12 rows, dec 1 st at each end of every row. 186[200:218:232] sts. Cast/bind off evenly.

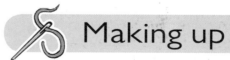

Making up

Sew in sleeves. Join side and sleeve seams.
Using matching or invisible thread, sew sequin trim all around lower edge of body and sleeves, then sew beads and sequins above trim as required.

Baby beanie

Hone your knitting skills with this tiny hat and have the cutest baby on the block.

Worked in a simple lace pattern, this is an ideal pull-on hat for babies and toddlers.

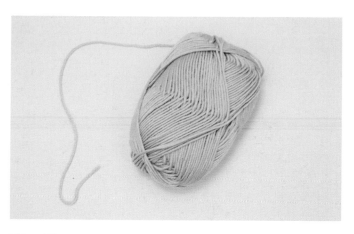

The Yarn

With its soft mix of pure wool, cashmere and microfibre, Debbie Bliss Baby Cashmerino is an ideal choice for baby garments – and it is machine washable as well. There is plenty of colour choice from traditional to contemporary baby shades.

GETTING STARTED

This simple hat is knitted in the easiest form of lace pattern consisting of eyelet holes formed by winding the yarn over the needle to make a stitch and then working two stitches together to keep the number of stitches correct.

Size:

To fit head circumferance: *38[41]cm/15[16in]*

Note: *Figures in square brackets [ ] refer to larger sizes; where there is only one set of figures, it applies to all sizes*

How much yarn:

1 x 50g (2oz) ball of Debbie Bliss Baby Cashmerino, approx 125m (137 yards) per ball

Needles:

Pair of 3mm (no. 11/US 2) knitting needles
Pair of 3.75mm (no. 9/US 5) knitting needles

Tension/gauge:

24 sts and 31 rows measure 10cm (4in) square over patt on 3.75mm (no. 9/US 5) needles
IT IS ESSENTIAL TO WORK TO THE STATED TENSION /GAUGE TO ACHIEVE SUCCESS

What you have to do:

Decorative increasing and decreasing to make eyelet pattern. Decrease stitches to shape crown of hat.

Instructions

Abbreviations:

alt = alternate;
beg = beginning;
cm = centimetre(s);
cont = continue;
foll = follow(s)(ing);
k = knit;
p = purl; **patt** = pattern;
rep = repeat;
rem = remaining;
RS = right side;
st(s) = stitch(es);
st st = stocking/stockinette stitch;
tog = together;
yfwd = yarn forward/yarn over between sts to make a st

BEANIE HAT:

With 3mm (no. 11/US 2) needles cast on 91[98] sts.
Beg with a K row, work 8[10] rows in st st.
Change to 3.75mm (no. 9/US 5) needles.
Cont in eyelet patt as foll:
1st row: (RS) K to end.
2nd and foll alt rows: P to end.
3rd row: *K5, yfwd, k2tog, rep from * to end.
5th row: K to end.
7th row: K2, *yfwd, k2tog, k5, rep from * ending last rep, k3.
8th row: P to end.
Cont in patt until work measures 12[14]cm/4¾[5½]in from 4th[5th] row worked on roll edge, ending with a 2nd or 6th patt row.

Shape crown:

1st row: K1, (k2tog, k4) 15[16] times, k0[1]. 76[82] sts.
2nd and foll alt rows: P to end.
3rd row: K1, (k2tog, k3) 15[16] times, k0[1]. 61[66] sts.
5th row: K1, (k2tog, k2) 15[16] times, k0[1]. 46[50] sts.
7th row: K1, (k2tog, k1) 15[16] times, k0[1]. 31[34] sts.
9th row: K1, (k2tog) 15[16] times, k0[1]. 16[18] sts.
11th row: (K2tog) to end. 8[9] sts.
Cut off yarn, leaving a long end.
Thread cut end through rem sts, draw up tight and fasten off securely.

STALK:

With 3mm (no. 11/US 2) needles cast on 6 sts. Work 6 rows in st st. Cast/bind off.

Making up

Join back seam, reversing seam on roll edge. Join cast-on and cast/bound-off edges of stalk, then attach stalk to top of hat.

HOW TO
MAKE A SIMPLE EYELET PATTERN

This pattern is created by winding the yarn round the needle to make a stitch and then knitting 2 stitches together to make a hole. This increasing and decreasing keeps the number of stitches the same.

1 The basic stitch is stocking/stockinette stitch. To make the eyelet pattern on a knit row, bring the yarn to the front when instructed.

2 Take the yarn over the needle, forming a loop, to knit the next two stitches together.

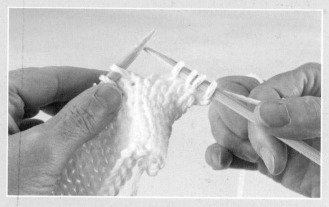

3 Completing this stitch forms a small hole, which becomes the eyelet. Continue in pattern to the end of the row.

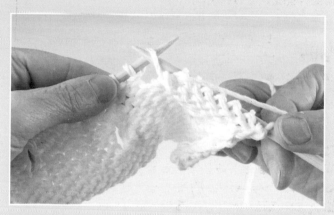

4 Alternate rows are worked in purl stitch. The yfwd movement in the previous row creates a stitch that is just looped over the needle. Purl in the usual way.

5 The positioning of the yfwd and k2 tog sequence in the eight rows that form the pattern ensures that the eyelet holes are offset.

Striped throw

Suitable for a beginner, this throw is bright and funky and perfect for a child's bedroom.

Bold and fun, this striking throw in a double knitting yarn combines squares of solid-coloured garter stitch with two-colour stripes in a simple openwork pattern.

GETTING STARTED

Squares are in basic stitches and sewing just five panels together is easier than lots of individual squares

Size:

Throw measures 100cm x 140cm (40in x 55in)

How much yarn:

3 x 50g (2oz) balls of Patons Diploma Gold DK, approx 120m (131 yards) per ball, in each of three colours A, B and E

4 balls in each of another two colours C and D

Needles:

Pair of 4mm (no. 8/US 6) knitting needles

Tension/gauge:

20 sts and 40 rows measure 10cm (4in) square over g st; 20 sts and 34 rows measure 10cm (4in) square over patt on 4mm (no. 8/US 6) needles

IT IS ESSENTIAL TO WORK TO THE STATED TENSION/GAUGE TO ACHIEVE SUCCESS

What you have to do:

Work throw in five long panels each containing seven squares. Panels consist of alternating garter stitch (every row knit) squares in a solid colour alternating with two-coloured striped squares in an openwork pattern. Following the diagram, sew the panels together with a flat seam.

The Yarn

Patons Diploma Gold DK is a mixture of 55% wool, 25% acrylic and 20% nylon. It combines the good looks of wool with the practicalities of synthetic fibres and it can be machine washed on a wool programme. There are plenty of shades to choose from for interesting colour combinations.

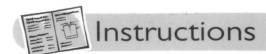 Instructions

Abbreviations:
cm = centimetre(s);
cont = continue; **k** = knit;
patt = pattern;
RS = right side;
st(s) = stitch(es);
tog = together;
yfwd = yarn forward/yarn
over to make a stitch

1st PANEL:

With C, cast on 40 sts. K 80 rows. Cont in patt as foll:
1st row: (RS) With D, k to end.
2nd row: With D, k1, (k2tog) to last st, k1. 21 sts.
3rd row: With D, k1, (yfwd, k1) to last st, k1. 40 sts.
4th row: With D, k to end.
5th row: With C, k to end.
6th row: With C, k1, (k2tog) to last st, k1. 21 sts.
7th row: With C, k2, (yfwd, k1) to end. 40 sts.
8th row: With C, k to end.
These 8 rows form patt. Patt 60 rows more, ending with 4 rows in D. Cut off D. With C, k 80 rows.
Working 1st–4th rows in A and 5th–8th rows in C, patt 68 rows. With C, k 80 rows.
Working 1st–4th rows in D and 5th–8th rows in C, patt 68 rows. With C, k 80 rows. Cast/bind off with C.

2ND PANEL:

With C, cast on 40 sts.
Working 1st–4th rows in C and 5th–8th rows in D, patt 68 rows. With D, k 80 rows.
Working 1st–4th rows in E and 5th–8th rows in D, patt 68 rows. With D, k 80 rows.
Working 1st–4th rows in B and 5th–8th rows in D, patt 68 rows.

With D, k 80 rows.
Working 1st–4th rows in C and 5th–8th rows in D, patt 68 rows.
Cast/bind off with C.

3RD PANEL:

With B, cast on 40 sts.
K 80 rows.
Working 1st–4th rows in D and 5th–8th rows in B, patt 68 rows. With B, k 80 rows.
Working 1st–4th rows in A and 5th–8th rows in B, patt 68 rows. With B, k 80 rows.
Working 1st–4th rows in D and 5th–8th rows in B, patt 68 rows. With B, k 80 rows. Cast/bind off with B.

4TH PANEL:

With C, cast on 40 sts.
Working 1st–4th rows in C and 5th–8th rows in A, patt 68 rows. With A, k 80 rows.
Working 1st–4th rows in E and 5th–8th rows in A, patt 68 rows. With A, k 80 rows.
Working 1st–4th rows in B and 5th–8th rows in A, patt 68 rows. With A, k 80 rows.
Working 1st–4th rows in C and 5th–8th rows in A, patt 68 rows. Cast/bind off with C.

5TH PANEL:

With E, cast on 40 sts. K 80 rows.

Working 1st–4th rows in D and 5th–8th rows in E, patt 68 rows.

With E, k 80 rows.

Working 1st–4th rows in A and 5th–8th rows in E, patt 68 rows.

With E, k 80 rows.

Working 1st–4th rows in D and 5th–8th rows in E, patt 68 rows.

With E, k 80 rows. Cast/bind off with E.

 Making up

Using a flat seam, join panels together following the diagram.

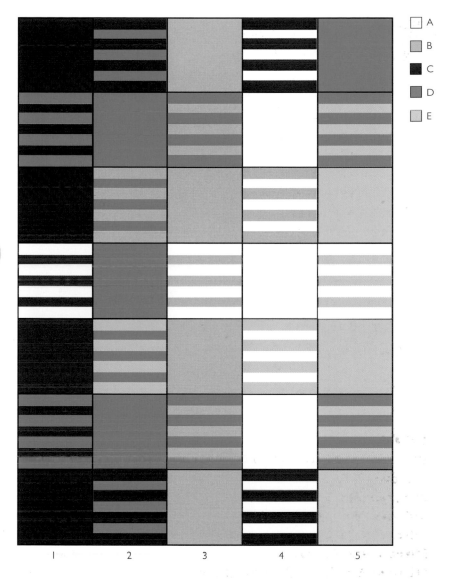

	A
	B
	C
	D
	E

Luxurious pencil case

Make this triangular-shaped case in soft angora yarn and use it to store your favourite pens and pencils.

Lined with a floral fabric, this handy zipped bag is the ultimate pencil case – or use it to store make-up or jewellery instead.

The Yarn

The yarn is from Orkney Angora and is a luxurious natural fibre called 'St Magnus' 50/50 DK – a blend of lambswool and angora that is soft and silky with a brushed appearance. It is available in a range of fabulous colours as well.

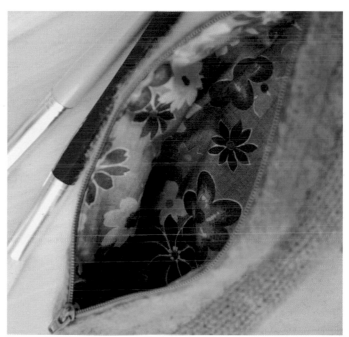

GETTING STARTED

 Simple stocking/stockinette stitch fabric with a basic cable trim and easy shaping

Size:
Case is 20cm long x 9.5cm high x 10cm deep
(8in x 3¾in x 4in)

How much yarn:
1 x 50g (2oz) ball of Orkney Angora 'St Magnus' 50/50 DK, approx 200m (219 yards) per ball

Needles:
Pair of 4.5mm (no. 7/US 7) knitting needles
Cable needle

Additional items:
40cm x 36cm (15¾in x 14in) piece of fabric for lining
Matching sewing thread, sewing needle and pins
20cm (8in) zip fastener

Tension/gauge:
21 sts and 28 rows to 10cm (4in) in st st on 4.5mm (no. 7/US 7) needles
IT IS ESSENTIAL TO WORK TO THE STATED TENSION/GAUGE TO ACHIEVE SUCCESS

What you have to do:
Work in st st. Increase by making a stitch (m1). Work basic cables. Sew a fabric lining. Sew in a zip fastener.

 # Instructions

PENCIL CASE:

Note: The pencil case is worked in one piece.
With 4.5mm (no. 7/US 7) needles, cast on 5 sts for end section.

1st row: (RS) K to end.
2nd row: P to end.
3rd row: K1, m1, k to last st, m1, k1. 7 sts.
4th row: P to end.
5th –16th rows: Rep 3rd and 4th rows 6 times more. 19 sts.
17th row: K to end.
18th row: P to end.
19th row: Rep 3rd row. 21 sts.
20th row: P to end.
21st row: K to end.

Abbreviations:

cm = centimetre(s);
cont = continue;
C4B = cable 4 back: sl next 2 sts on to cable needle and leave at back of work, k2, then k2 from cable needle;
C4F = cable 4 front: sl next 2 sts on to cable needle and leave at front of work, k2, then k2 from cable needle;
foll = follow(s)(ing);
k = knit; **m1** = make 1 st by picking up horizontal loop lying between needles and working into back of it;
p = purl;
psso = pass slipped st over;
rem = remain;
rep = repeat;
RS = right side; **sl** = slip;
st(s) = stitch(es);
st st = stocking/ stockinette stitch;
tog = together;
WS = wrong side

Tip: Before making up the pencil case, first hand wash the knitted piece and leave it to dry naturally to bring out the character of the yarn. When dry, brush gently to fluff up the pile.

22nd row: P to end, turn and cast on 20 sts.

Centre section:

1st row: K4, p1, k4, p1, k to end. Cast on 20 sts on empty needle with short length of yarn, then cont across cast-on sts as foll: k10, p1, k4, p1, k4.
2nd row: P4, k1, p4, k1, p to last 10 sts, k1, p4, k1, p4.
3rd row: K4, p1, k4, p1, k to last 10 sts, p1, k4, p1, k4.
4th row: As 2nd row.
5th row: K4, p1, C4F, p1, k to last 10 sts, p1, C4B, p1, k4.
Rep 2nd –5th rows 13 times more, then work 2nd–4th rows again.

End section:

Next row: Cast/bind off 20 sts, k21, Cast/ bind off rem 20 sts. Cut off yarn. Turn work, rejoin yarn and cont as foll:
1st row: P to end.
2nd row: K to end.
3rd row: P to end.
4th row: Sl1, k1, psso, k to last 2 sts, k2tog.
5th –8th rows: As 1st to 4th rows.
Rep 3rd and 4th rows until 5 sts rem.
Next row: P to end.
Cast/bind off.

Making up

Lining: Lay the knitted piece out flat on top of the lining fabric. Draw around it, marking two more lines around – one 5mm (¼in) side (sewing line) and the other 5mm (¼in) outside (cutting line). Cut out lining. Fold a 5mm (¼in) double hem to the WS along the tops of the end sections and sew in place. With RS facing, stitch along end seams. Fold a 1cm (⅜in) turning to WS around rest of opening edges and tack/baste in place. Using backstitch, join end seams of knitted bag. Turn to RS. Insert lining in bag. Pin, tack/baste and then sew zip fastener in place, between the lining and knitted case.

HOW TO
INCREASE A STITCH WITHIN A ROW

Stitches are added to the row in this pattern with a technique called invisible raised increasing. In a pattern this is described as 'make 1 stitch' using the abbreviation m1.

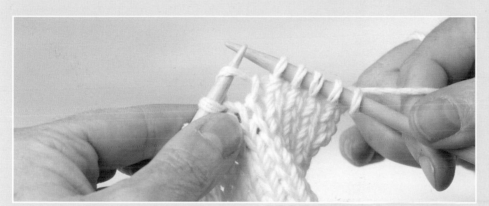

1 To make 1 stitch in a knit row, when you reach the instructed point in the row open out the two needles slightly. A strand of yarn stretches horizontally between the two needles. Put the tip of the left-hand needle under this strand from front to back.

2 Work into the back of the lifted strand as shown in the photograph below.

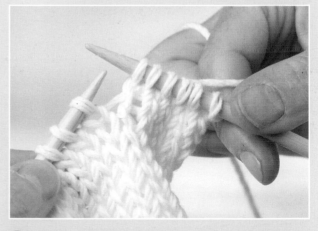

3 Wrap the yarn around the right-hand needle in the usual way and pull the stitch back through the loop, sliding the stitch off the left-hand needle. You will have created an extra stitch on the right-hand needle.

Cool kid's sweater

A classic design is adapted to make a great kid's sweater that's brilliant for boys and girls.

For trendy tots to wear with their denims, this classic sweater with ribbed front opening and collar is easy to knit in stocking/stockinette stitch.

GETTING STARTED

Simple drop-shoulder style sweater in stocking/ stockinette stitch with the minimum of shaping

Sizes:

To fit chest: 46[51:56:61:66]cm/18[20:22:24:26]in
Actual size: 51[56:62:65:71]cm/20[22:24½:25½:28¼]in
Length: 28[32:38:42:48]cm/11[12½:15:16½:19]in
Sleeve seam: 17[20:24:29:33]cm/6¾[8:9½:11½:13]in
Note: *Figures in square brackets [ ] refer to larger sizes; where there is only one set of figures, it applies to all sizes*

How much yarn:

2[3:3:4:5] x 50g (2oz) balls of Sirdar Snuggly DK, approx 165m (180 yards) per ball

Needles:

Pair of 3.25mm (no. 10/US 3) knitting needles
Pair of 4mm (no. 8/US 6) knitting needles

Additional items:

Stitch holder

Tension/gauge:

22 sts and 28 rows measure 10cm (4in) square over st st on 4mm (no. 8/US 6) needles
IT IS ESSENTIAL TO WORK TO THE STATED TENSION/GAUGE TO ACHIEVE SUCCESS

What you have to do:

Work in k2, p2 rib. Work main fabric in stocking/ stockinette stitch. Divide front for opening and work each side separately. Pick up stitches for opening edges and around neck for collar. 'Make 1' to increase stitches on collar edge.

The Yarn

Sirdar Snuggly DK is a mixture of 55% nylon and 45% acrylic making it light, soft and hard-wearing – so perfect for babies and children. It can be machine washed and is available in a full range of pastel and 'grown-up' colours for contemporary kids.

 Instructions

BACK:

With 3.25mm (no. 10/US 3) needles cast on 62[66:74:78:86] sts.
1st row: K2, *p2, k2, rep from * to end.
2nd row: P2, *k2, p2, rep from * to end.
Work 3[5:5:5:5] more rows in rib as set.
Next row: Rib 5[8:6:8:7], rib 2 tog, (rib 8[14:10:10:8], rib 2 tog) 5[3:5:5:7] times, rib 5[8:6:8:7]. 56[62:68:72:78] sts.
Change to 4mm (no. 8/US 6) needles. **
Beg with a k row, cont in st st until Back measures 28[32:38:42:48]cm/11[12½:15:16½:19]in from beg, ending with a WS row.

Shape shoulders:

Cast/bind off 9[10:11:11:13] sts at beg of next 2 rows and 9[10:12:12:13] sts at beg of foll 2 rows. Cast/bind off rem 20[22:22:26:26] sts.

FRONT:

Work as given for Back to **.
Beg with a k row, cont in st st until Front measures 18[20:25:29:35]cm/7[8:10:11½:13¾]in from beg, ending

Abbreviations:

alt = alternate;
beg = beginning;
cm = centimetre(s);
cont = continue;
dec = decrease(ing);
foll = follow(s)(ing);
inc = increase(ing);
k = knit; **p** = purl;
rem = remain(ing);
rep = repeat;
RS = right side;
st(s) = stitch(es);
st st = stocking/stockinette stitch;
tog = together;
WS = wrong side

with a WS row.

Divide for front opening:
Next row: K26[29:32:34:37], turn and leave rem sts on a holder. Complete this side of neck first.

*** Next row: P to end.

1st, 4th and 5th sizes only:
Work 4 rows, dec 1 st at end of next and foll alt row. 24[32:35] sts.

All sizes:
Work 7[17:17:13:13] rows, dec 1 st at end of 3rd[1st:1st:1st:1st] and every foll 4th row. 22[24:27:28:31] sts. Work 4 rows straight.

Shape neck:
Next row: Cast/bind off 1[1:1:2:2] sts, p to end. Work 5 rows, dec 1 st at neck edge on next and every foll alt row. 18[20:23:23:26] sts. Work straight to match Back to shoulder, ending at armhole edge.

Shape shoulder:
Cast/bind off 9[10:11:11:13] sts at beg of next work. Work 1 row. Cast/bind off rem 9[10:12:12:13] sts. With RS facing, rejoin yarn to rem sts, cast/bind off centre 4 sts, k to end. 26[29:32:34:37] sts. Complete as given for other side of neck from *** to end, reversing shaping.

SLEEVES: (Make 2)
With 3.25mm (no. 10/US 3) needles cast on 38[38:42: 46:46] sts. Work 5[7:7:7:7] rows in k2, p2 rib as given for Back.
Next row: Rib to end, dec 2 sts evenly across row for 1st, 3rd and 4th sizes only. 36[38:40:44:46] sts. Change to 4mm (no. 8/US 6) needles. Beg with a k row, cont in st st, inc 1 st at each end of 7th[7th:9th:9th:9th] and every foll 8th row to 44[48:52:52:54] sts.

4th and 5th sizes only:
Inc 1 st at each end of every foll 10th row to [58:62] sts.

All sizes:
Work straight until Sleeve measures 17[20:24:29:33]cm/6¾[8:9½:11½:13]in from beg, ending with a WS row.

Shape sleeve top:
Cast/bind off 4 sts at beg of next 2[8:4:8:4] rows and 5 sts at beg of foll 6[2:6:4:8] rows. Cast/bind off rem 6 sts.

FRONT EDGINGS: (Alike)
With 3.25mm (no. 10/US 3) needles and RS of work facing, pick up and k20[28:28:28:28] sts evenly along shaped edge of opening.
1st row: K1, *p2, k2, rep from * to last 3 sts, p3.
2nd row: P1, *k2, p2, rep from * to last 3 sts, k2, p1. Work 3 more rows in rib as set. Cast/bind off in rib.

COLLAR:
Join shoulder seams.
With 3.25mm (no. 10/US 3) needles, RS of work facing and beg at edge of front edging, pick up and k25[26:28:28:30] sts up right front neck, 20[22:22:26:26] sts

HOW TO
USE A STITCH HOLDER

Stitch holders are a useful tool for the knitter and are constructed like a giant safety pin. They come in a variety of lengths and you can select the holder according to the number of stitches that you need to store on it.

1 Knit to the instructed point in the row. Open the stitch holder and slide the needle end under each stitch on the left-hand needle. Keeping the stitches the right way round, take them onto the holder. Clip the holder shut.

2 Continue knitting the stitches remaining on the right-hand needle for the instructed length and then cast/bind off.

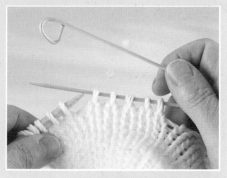

3 Open the stitch holder and slide the stitches, one by one, onto the left-hand needle. Again, be careful not to twist the stitches.

4 Join in the yarn on the right-hand edge and knit the remaining stitches for the instructed length.

5 This is the effect created by working two sets of stitches separately. In this pattern it is used to create the neck opening.

---

from back neck and 25[26:28:28:30] sts down left front neck, ending at edge of front edging. 70[74:78:82:86] sts. Beg with 1st row, work 12[14:16:18:18] rows in k2, p2 rib as Back.
Next row: *K2, p1, pick up loop lying between needles and make st by purling into back of it, p1, rep from * to last 2 sts, k2. 87[92:97:102:107] sts.
Next row: P2, *k3, p2, rep from * to end.
Cast/bind off in rib.

Making up

Mark positions of underarms with pins about 12[13:14:15:16]cm/4¾[5:5½:6:6¼]in down from shoulders. Sew in sleeves between markers, matching centre of top to shoulder seams. Join side and sleeve seams. Placing right over left for a girl or left over right for a boy, join side edges of front edging to cast/bound-off sts at centre front neck. Pin out garment to given measurements. Cover with slightly damp cloths and leave until dry.

Heart-motif baby blanket

The softest yarn and a delightful design make this blanket the perfect baby companion.

Featuring textured and coloured hearts on a stocking/stockinette stitch background with cable panels, this blanket will make a treasured gift for a baby.

GETTING STARTED

 Complex colour and texture pattern worked entirely from a chart is worth the challenge for an experienced knitter

Size:
Blanket measures 73cm x 84cm (28¾in x 33in)

How much yarn:
9 x 50g (2oz) balls of Sirdar Snuggly Baby Bamboo DK, approx 95m (104 yards) per ball, in colour A – cream 3 balls in colour B – blue

Needles:
4mm (no. 8/US 6) circular knitting needle
Cable needle

Tension/gauge:
22 sts and 28 rows measure 10cm (4in) square over stocking/stockinette stitch on 4mm (no. 8/US 6) needles IT IS ESSENTIAL TO WORK TO THE STATED TENSION/ GAUGE TO ACHIEVE SUCCESS

What you have to do:
Use circular needle to work large number of stitches in rows. Work cast-on and cast/bound-off edges in rib. Follow chart for pattern. using intarsia technique for cable panels and small hearts in a second colour.

Abbreviations:

cm = centimetre(s); **cont** = continue; **foll** = follow;
k = knit; **p** = purl; **patt** = pattern; **rem** = remain(ing);
rep = repeat; **RS** = right side; **st(s)** = stitch(es);
tbl = through back of **loop; tog** = together; **WS** = wrong
side **C4B** = cable 4 back as foll: slip next 2 sts on to a
cable needle and leave at back of work, k2, then k 2 sts
from cable needle **Tw2R** = twist 2 right as foll: slip next st
onto cable needle and leave at back of work, slip next st
purlwise, then k1 tbl from cable needle

Notes:

When working from chart, read odd-numbered (RS) rows
from right to left and even-numbered (WS) rows from left
to right. Use small separate balls of A and B for each area
of colour, twisting yarns tog on WS of work when changing
colour to avoid holes forming.

The Yarn

Sirdar Snuggy Baby Bamboo DK is a natural blend of 80% bamboo and 20% wool. The yarn has a light twist and subtle sheen that are very attractive and it can be machine washed. There are plenty of shades in pastel and deep contemporary colours to choose from.

 # Instructions

BLANKET:

With 4mm (no. 8/US 6) circular needle and A, cast on
167 sts. Working forwards and back in rows, cont in
rib as foll:
1st rib row: (RS) K2, (p1, k2) to end.
2nd rib row: P2, (k1, p2) to end.
Rep these 2 rows twice more.
Cont in patt from chart as foll:
1st row: (RS) P6 A, *(k17 A, p1 B, k4 B, p1 B) twice,
rep from * twice more, k17 A, p6 A.
2nd row: P23 A, *(k1 B, p4 B, k1 B, p17 A) twice, rep
from * twice more, p6 A.
Cont in patt from chart as set until all 80 rows have
been completed, then work 33rd–48th rows. Rep last
96 rows once more and finally work 1st–32nd rows
again. 224 rows in total. Cont in A only, work 6 more
rows in rib. Cast/bind off in rib.

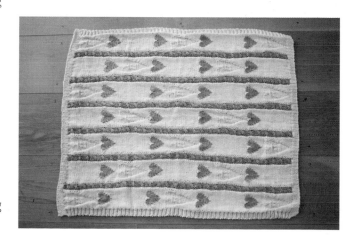

Making up

Carefully darn in yarn ends on WS of work. If required press with a cool iron over a dry cloth taking care not to flatten pattern.

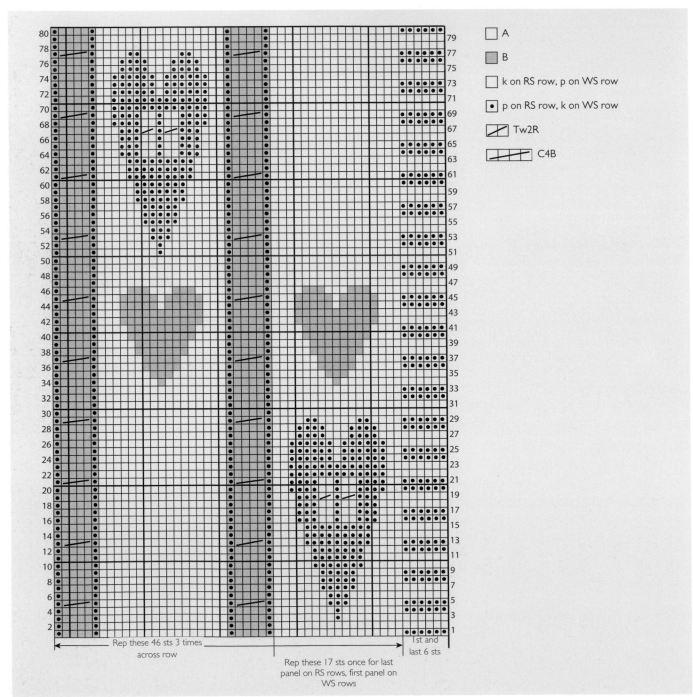

□ A

■ B

□ k on RS row, p on WS row

• p on RS row, k on WS row

⧄ Tw2R

⧄ C4B

Rep these 46 sts 3 times across row

Rep these 17 sts once for last panel on RS rows, first panel on WS rows

1st and last 6 sts

Cat and mouse set

Take your pick from the hat, mitts and bootees or knit all three and play cat and mouse.

Worked in soft shades of baby yarn and easy stitches, this set of 'cat' hat and mittens with 'mouse' boots will add a touch of style to a little one's wardrobe.

The Yarn
Debbie Bliss Baby Cashmerino is a blend of 55% merino wool, 33% microfibre and 12% cashmere. It is very soft to touch and perfect for a baby's skin.

There is a wide colour palette and the yarn can be machine washed at a low temperature.

GETTING STARTED

 Easy stitches and shaping but pay attention to details for good results

Size:
Hat to fit age: *3–6[6–9:9–12] months*
Actual size: *36[39:42]cm/14[15¼:16½]in circumference*
Mittens to fit age: *0–6[6–12] months*
Boots to fit age: *0–6[6–12] months*
Note: *Figures in square brackets [ ] refer to larger sizes; where there is only one set of figures, it applies to all sizes*

How much yarn:
1 x 50g (2oz) ball of Debbie Bliss Baby Cashmerino, approx 125m (137 yards) per ball, in colour A – pale beige for Hat, colour B – dark beige for Mittens and colour C – camel for Boots

Needles:
Pair of 3.25mm (no. 10/US 3) knitting needles
Spare 3.25mm (no. 10/US 3) knitting needle

Additional items:
2 x four-hole medium brown buttons
4 x four-hole small brown buttons
4 x brown wooden beads
Scraps of brown felt and dark brown embroidery thread (floss)

Tension/gauge:
25 sts and 34 rows measure 10cm (4in) square over st st on 3.25mm (no. 10/US 3) needles
IT IS ESSENTIAL TO WORK TO THE STATED TENSION /GAUGE TO ACHIEVE SUCCESS

What you have to do:
Work all pieces in stocking/stockinette stitch with rolled hems. Use simple shaping throughout as instructed. Make separate ear pieces and sew on. Sew on buttons for eyes and felt or embroidery for nose. Make whiskers from long strands of yarn.

Abbreviations:

alt = alternate;
beg = beginning;
cm = centimetre(s);
cont = continue;
dec = decrease(ing);
foll = following;
inc = increase(ing);
k = knit;
m1 = make one stitch by picking up strand lying between needles and working into back of it;
p = purl;
psso = pass slipped stitch over;
rem = remain(ing);
rep = repeat;
RS = right side;
sl = slip; **st(s)** = stitch(es);
st st = stocking/stockinette stitch;
tbl = through back of loops;
tog = together;
WS = wrong side

Instructions

HAT:

With A, cast on 90[98: 106] sts. Beg with a k row, cont in st st until work measures 10.5[11:11]cm/4[4¼:4¼]in from beg, ending with a WS row.

Shape crown:

1st dec row: K1, (k9[10:11], k2tog) 8 times, k1. 82[90:98] sts.
Beg with a p row, work 3 rows in st st.
2nd dec row: K1, (k8[9:10], k2tog) 8 times, k1. 74[82:90] sts.
Beg with a p row, work 3 rows in st st.
3rd dec row: K1, (k7[8:9], k2tog) 8 times, k1. 66[74:82] sts. P 1 row.
4th dec row: K1, (k6[7:8], k2tog) 8 times, k1. 58[66:74] sts. P 1 row.
5th dec row: K1, (k5[6:7], k2tog) 8 times, k1. 50[58:66] sts. P 1 row.
6th dec row: K1, (k4[5:6], k2tog) 8 times, k1. 42[50:58] sts. P 1 row.
7th dec row: K1, (k3[4:5], k2tog) 8 times, k1. 34[42:50] sts. P 1 row.
8th dec row: K1, (k2[3:4], k2tog) 8 times, k1. 26[34:42] sts. P 1 row.
9th dec row: K1, (k1[2:3], k2tog) 8 times, k1. 18[26:34] sts.

2nd size only:

P 1 row.
10th dec row: K1, (k1, k2tog) 8 times, k1. 18 sts.

3rd size only:

P 1 row.
10th dec row: K1, (k2, k2tog) 8 times, k1. 26 sts. P 1 row.
11th dec row: K1, (k1, k2tog) 8 times, k1. 18 sts.

All sizes:

Next row: P1, (p2tog) 8 times, p1. 10 sts. Cut off yarn,

leaving a long end for sewing back seam. Thread cut end through rem sts, draw up tightly and fasten off.

EARS: (Make 4)

With A, cast on 16 sts. Beg with a k row, work 2 rows in st st.
Next row: K1, sl 1, k1, psso, k to last 3 sts, k2tog, k1.
P 1 row. Rep last 2 rows until 4 sts rem.
Next row: Sl 1, k1, psso, k2tog.
Next row: P2tog, cut off yarn, thread through rem st and fasten off.

MITTENS:
Right mitten:

* With B, cast on 29[33] sts. Beg with a k row, work 4 rows in st st.
Next row: K1, (p1, k1) to end.
Next row: P1, (k1, p1) to end.
Rep last 2 rows once more. Beg with a k row, work 2 rows in st st. *

Shape thumb:

Next row: K15[17], m1, k1, m1, k13[15]. P 1 row.
Next row: K15[17], m1, k3, m1, k13[15].
Cont in this way, inc 2 sts in centre on foll alt rows until there are 39[43] sts. P 1 row.

Divide for thumb:

Next row: K26[28], turn.
Next row: Cast on 1 st, p12, turn.
Next row: Cast on 1 st, k to end. 13 sts.
**Beg with a p row, work 5[7] rows on these 13 sts only.
Next row: (K2tog) twice, sl 1, k2tog, psso, (k2tog)
3 times. Cut off yarn, thread through rem 6 sts, pull up tightly and secure. Join thumb seam.
With RS of work facing, rejoin yarn at base of thumb and pick up and k 3 sts from base of thumb, k to end. 31[35] sts. Beg with a p row, work 7[9] rows in st st.

Shape top:
Next row: K1, (sl 1, k1, psso, k10[12], k2tog, k1) twice.
Beg with a p row, work 3 rows in st st.
Next row: K1, (sl 1, k1, psso, k8[10], k2tog, k1) twice.
P 1 row.
Next row: K1, (sl 1, k1, psso, k6[8], k2tog, k1) twice.

1st size only:
P 1 row.

2nd size only:
Next row: P1, (p2tog, p6, p2tog tbl, p1) twice.

Both sizes:
Next row: K1, (sl 1, k1, psso, k4, k2tog, k1) twice.
Next row: P1, (p2tog, p2, p2tog tbl, p1) twice.
Cast/bind off rem 11 sts.

Left mitten:
Work as given for Right mitten from * to *.

Shape thumb:
Next row: K13[15], m1, k1, m1, k15[17]. P 1 row.
Next row: K13[15], m1, k3, m1, k15[17].
Cont in this way, inc 2 sts in centre on foll alt rows until
there are 39[43] sts. P 1 row.

Divide for thumb:
Next row: K24[26], turn.
Next row: Cast on 1 st, p12, turn.
Next row: Cast on 1 st, k to end. 13 sts.
Complete as given for Left mitten from ** to end.

EARS: (Make 4)
With B, cast on 3 sts.
Beg with a k row, work 2 rows in st st.
Next row: K1, (m1, k1) twice. 5 sts. P 1 row.
Next row: K1, m1, k3, m1, k1. 7 sts.
Beg with a p row, work 3 rows in st st.
Next row: K1, sl 1, k1, psso, k1, k2tog, k1. 5 sts.
P 1 row. Cast/bind off.

BOOTS: (Make 2)
With C, cast on 25[35] sts.
1st and foll alt rows: (RS) K to end.
2nd row: K1, m1, k11[16], m1, k1, m1, k11[16], m1, k1.
4th row: K2, m1, k11[16], m1, k3, m1, k11[16], m1, k2.
6th row: K3, m1, k11[16], m1, k5, m1, k11[16], m1, k3.
Cont in this way, inc 4 sts as set on every foll alt row,
until there are 49[59] sts. K 1 row and p 1 row.
Shape nose:
Next row: K24[29], m1, k1, m1, k24[29]. P 1 row.
Next row: K25[30], m1, k1, m1, k25[30]. P 1 row.
Next row: K26[31], m1, k1, m1, k26[31]. P 1 row.
Next row: K27[32], m1, k1, m1, k27[32]. 57[67] sts.
Beg with a p row, work 3 rows in st st.
Toe seam and shape upper:
Next row: K1, (sl 1, k1, psso) twice, k23[28], with spare
3.25mm (no. 10/US 3) needle k centre st, then fold piece
in half at centre point with WS facing so that original
pair of needles are parallel to each other in left hand;
with spare needle, k 1 st from front needle tog with
corresponding st on back needle and cast/bind it off using
st already on spare needle; cont in this way until 22[25]
sts rem on front needle only; using spare needle (holding
1 st), k17[20], (k2tog) twice, k1 from front left-hand
needle only, turn.
Next row: (working across both needles) P18[21],
p2tog, p1, p2tog tbl, p18[21]. 39[45] sts.
Next row: K1, (sl 1, k1, psso) twice, k12[15], sl 1, k1,
psso, k1, k2tog, k12[15], (k2tog) twice, k1. P 1 row.
Next row: K1, sl 1, k1, psso, k11[14], sl 1, k1, psso, k1,
k2tog, k11[14], k2tog, k1. P 1 row.
Next row: K12[15], sl 1, k1, psso, k1, k2tog, k12[15].
27[33] sts.

Beg with a p row, work 5 rows in st st. Cast/bind off.
EARS: (Make 4)
Using yarn C, work as given for Mittens.

 ## Making up

HAT:

Join centre back seam, reversing seam for last 3cm
(1¼in) at hem. Sew each pair of ears tog with WS
facing, then sew cast-on edges of each ear to top of hat
approximately 2cm (¾in) from centre of crown and
with each cast-on edge either side of decrease lines.
Using the picture as a guide and dark brown embroidery
thread, sew two button 'eyes' just below start of
decreasing. Cut a small triangle of brown felt for 'nose'
and sew this centrally between the eyes. With yarn C,
thread 8 'whiskers' (four each side of nose) through
knitted fabric and knot at back to secure.

MITTENS:

Sew cast/bound-off edge of each ear to top of each
mitten 2cm (¾in) below cuff. Then sew button 'eyes'
just below ears using dark brown embroidery thread.
Cut two small triangles of brown felt for 'noses' and sew
to each mitten below button eyes.
With yarn C, thread 8 'whiskers' (four each side of nose)
to each mitten through knitted fabric and knot at back
to secure. Join side seams of mittens, reversing seam for
roll back stocking/stockinette stitch above ribbed cuff.

BOOTS:

Join centre back, heel and sole seam, reversing seam for
approximately 2cm (¾in) at top edge for roll back cuff.
Sew cast/bound-off edge of each ear to top of shoe,
either side of centre stitch and just below cuff. Using
dark brown embroidery thread, sew on beads for 'eyes'
just below ears. Using embroidery thread and satin
stitch, embroider triangle for 'nose' at tip of toe seam.
With yarn C, thread 8 'whiskers' (four each side of nose)
through knitted fabric and knot at back to secure.

Loretta Lamb

Who can resist the charms of Loretta Lamb? She's soft, sweet, and adorable and just made for cuddling.

With her 'square' shape, sweet expression and 'shrunken' dress, this cute lamb has real cuddle appeal. Knitted throughout in stocking/ stockinette stitch, she has separate head, body, arms and legs that are sewn together, and a striped dress.

The Yarn
Debbie Bliss Baby Cashmerino is a blend of 55% merino wool, 33% microfibre and 12% cashmere in a 4-ply (fingering) weight. The combination of beautiful natural fibres with a man-made one creates a yarn that is soft and ideal for babies, yet practical at the same time. There is a fabulous colour range to select from so you could choose plenty of other colourways for the lamb's dress.

GETTING STARTED

 Easy stitches and techniques but the toy consists of quite a few small and fiddly pieces

Size:
Toy is approximately 28cm (11in) in height

How much yarn:
1 x 50g (2oz) ball of Debbie Bliss Baby Cashmerino, approx 125m (137 yards) per ball, in each of five colours A, B, C, D and E

Needles:
Pair of 3.25mm (no. 10/US 3) knitting needles

Additional items:
2 stitch holders
Polyester toy filling

Tension/gauge:
25 sts and 34 rows measure 10cm (4in) square over st st on 3.25mm (no. 10/US 3) needles
IT IS ESSENTIAL TO WORK TO THE STATED TENSION/GAUGE TO ACHIEVE SUCCESS

What you have to do:
Work mainly in stocking/stockinette stitch with paired shapings and turning rows. Make the body in sections, stuff with toy filling and sew them together. Knit dress in stripes of stocking/stockinette stitch.

Instructions

Abbreviations:
beg = beginning;
cm = centimetre(s);
cont = continue;
dec = decrease;
foll = follow(s)(ing);
m1 = make one stitch by picking up strand lying between needles and work into back of it;
k = knit; **p** = purl;
patt = pattern;
rem = remaining;
rep = repeat;
RS = right side;
st(s) = stitch(es);
st st = stocking/stockinette stitch;
tbl = through back of loops; **tog** = together;
WS = wrong side

HEAD:

With A, cast on 6 sts.

Next row: (RS) K1, k into front and then back of next 4 sts, k1. 10 sts. P1 row.

Next row: K1, k into front and then back of next 8 sts, k1. 18 sts. P1 row.

Next row: K into front and then back of every st to end. 36 sts. Beg with a p row, work 7 rows in st st.

Next row: K32, turn.

Next row: Wrap yarn round right-hand needle, p28, turn.

Next row: Wrap yarn round right-hand needle, k24, turn.

Next row: Wrap yarn round right-hand needle, p20, turn.

Next row: Wrap yarn round right-hand needle, k16, turn.

Next row: Wrap yarn round right-hand needle, p12, turn.

Next row: Wrap yarn round right-hand needle, k8, turn.

Next row: Wrap yarn round right-hand needle, p to end, working all extra loops tog tbl with foll st.

Next row: K to end, working all extra loops tog with foll st. Work 3 rows straight.

Next row: K9, k2tog tbl, k14, k2tog, k9. P1 row.

Next row: K9, k2tog tbl, k12, k2tog, k9. P1 row.

Next row: K9, k2tog tbl, k10, k2tog, k9.

Next row: P9, p2tog, p8, p2tog tbl, p9.

Next row: K9, k2tog tbl, k6, k2tog, k9.

Next row: P9, p2tog, p4, p2tog tbl, p9.

Next row: K9, k2tog tbl, k2, k2tog, k9. 22 sts

Next row: P2, (p2tog, p2) 5 times. 17 sts

Next row: K1, (k2tog) 8 times.

Cut off yarn and thread through rem 9 sts. Pull up tightly and fasten off.

EARS: (Make 2)

With A, cast on 5 sts.

Beg with a k row, cont in st st and work 2 rows.

Next row: K2, m1, k1, m1, k2. P1 row.

Next row: K3, m1, k1, m1, k3. P1 row.

Next row: K4, m1, k1, m1, k4. 11 sts

Work 9 rows straight.

Next row: K1, (k2tog) twice, k1, (k2tog) twice, k1. 7 sts. Cast/bind off purlwise.

LEGS: (Make 2)

With B, cast on 6 sts.

Inc row: (RS) K into front and then back of every st to end of row. P1 row.*

Rep last 2 rows twice more. 48 sts. Beg with a k row, work 4 rows in st st.

Dec row: (K2tog) 24 times. 24 sts.

P1 row. Cut off B and join in A. Beg with a k row, cont in st st and work 20 rows. Cast/bind off.

ARMS: (Make 2)

Work as for given for Legs to *.

Rep last 2 rows once more. 24 sts. Beg with a k row, work 4 rows in st st.

Cut off B and join in A. Cont in st st, dec 1 st at each end of next 3 rows. 18 sts. Work 19 rows straight. Cast/bind off.

BODY: (Make 2)

With A, cast on 25 sts. Mark centre st with a marker. Beg with a k row, cont in st st and work 2 rows.

Next row: (RS) K up to marked centre st, m1, k1 (centre st), m1, k to end. P1 row. Rep last 2 rows until there are 35 sts. Work 18 rows straight.

Next row: (RS) K4, (k2tog, k4) 5 times, k1. 30 sts. Work 3 rows straight.

Next row: K4, (k2tog, k3), 5 times, k1. 25 sts. Work 3 rows straight.

Next row: K3, (k2tog, k2) 5 times, k2. 20 sts. Work 3 rows straight.

Next row: K3, (k2tog, k1) 5 times, k2. 15 sts. P1 row.

Next row: K2, (k2tog) 5 times, k3. 10 sts. Cast/bind off.

DRESS:

Sleeves:

With E, cast on 23 sts.

1st row: (RS) K1, *p1, k1, rep from * to end.

2nd row: P1, *k1, p1, rep from * to end.

Cut off E and join in C.

Inc row: K3, k into front and back of next 17 sts, k3. 40 sts. Beg with a p row, work 9 rows in st st.

Dec row: (WS) K10, (k2tog) 10 times, k10. 30 sts. P1 row. Cast/bind off.

Front and back: (Alike)

With C, cast on 41 sts. Work 2 rows in k1, p1 rib as given for Sleeves. Beg with a k row, cont in st st and stripe patt of 4 rows E, 2 rows C, 4 rows D and 2 rows C. Keeping stripe patt correct, work as foll:

Next row: (RS) K5, (k2tog) 16 times, k4. 25 sts.

Work 11 rows straight.

Shape front neck:

Next row: (RS) K10, turn and complete this side of neck first. Dec 1 st at neck edge on next 4 rows. 6 sts. P1 row. Cast/bind off.

With RS facing, slip centre 5 sts on to a holder, rejoin yarn and k to end. Complete to match first side of neck.

Neck edging:

Join one shoulder seam.

With, D and RS of work facing, *pick up and k 7 sts down first side of neck,

k 5 sts from stitch holder, pick up and k 7 sts up second side of neck*, pick up and k one stitch from shoulder seam, rep from * to *. 39 sts. Beg with 2nd row, work 2 rows in rib as given for Sleeves. Cast/bind off in rib.

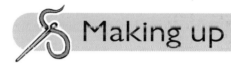

Making up

LAMB:

Join cast-on edge at back of head and first four rows at nose end of head. Stuff firmly. Sew on cast-off edge of ears to side of head, aligning them with start of front head shaping. With B, work two small French knots for eyes slightly below the ears. For the nose and mouth, work 2 small straight stitches with B in a V shape, following the front nose shaping. Below this work a small vertical and then a small horizontal straight stitch. Join seams on arms and legs and stuff firmly. Join lower and side edges of body pieces, enclosing top edges of arms and legs in the seams. Stuff firmly. Sew head securely to top edge of body.

DRESS:

Sew sleeves to sides of dress, matching centre of sleeves to shoulder seams. Join side and sleeve seams.

Child's backpack

Use a stunning multicoloured yarn to make this fun bag that stands out in the crowd.

This fabulous backpack-style bag is so distinctive that it's guaranteed never to get lost at school! It includes a matching purse that can be attached by a cord and popped inside.

GETTING STARTED

 Simple fabric and shaping, but working in the round and constructing bag requires attention

Size:
Backpack is approximately 22cm wide x 26cm tall x 7cm deep (8½in x 10¼in x 2¾in)
Purse is approximately 12cm x 8cm (4¾in x 3in)

How much yarn:
3 x 50g (2oz) hanks of Noro Blossom, approx 87m (95 yards) per hank

Needles:
Pair of 4mm (no. 8/US 6) knitting needles
4mm (no. 8/US 6) circular knitting needle in a short length

Additional items:
Stitch markers
2 buttons 18mm and 22mm (¾in and 1in)
2 press studs (popper snaps) 17mm (¾in)
2 strap buckles 25mm (1in)

Tension/gauge:
17 sts and 24 rows measure 10cm (4in) square over st st on 4mm (no. 8/US 6) needles
IT IS ESSENTIAL TO WORK TO THE STATED TENSION/ GAUGE TO ACHIEVE SUCCESS

What you have to do:
Use circular needle to cast on and work in rows of stocking/stockinette stitch, shaping at same time, for flap. Cast on extra stitches for top of bag front and continue working throughout in rounds. Graft stitches together at bottom of bag. Work straps in single (knit one, purl one) rib. Work separate purse in stocking/ stockinette stitch. Make twisted cords for eyelets at top of bag front and to attach purse. Strengthen long strap and make up bag following instructions.

The Yarn
Noro Blossom is a blend of 40% wool, 30% kid mohair, 20% silk and 10% nylon. It is a luxurious yarn with a rich textured effect in a mixture of delicious variegated shades that knit up to give a colourful striped effect. This yarn is hand wash only.

beg = beginning;
cm = centimetre(s);
cont = continue;
foll = follow(s)(ing);
inc = increase(ing);
k = knit; **p** = purl;
psso = pass slipped stitch over;
rem = remain(ing);
rep = repeat;
RS = right side; **sl** = slip;
st(s) = stitch(es);
st st = stocking/ stockinette stitch;
tog = together;
WS = wrong side;
yfwd = yarn forward/yarn over to make a stitch

Instructions

BAG:

With circular needle cast on 13 sts for flap. Working forwards and back in rows, cont as foll:

1st row: (RS) Inc in first st, k to last st, inc in last st.

2nd row: P to end.

Rep these 2 rows 9 times more. 33 sts. Now inc 1 st in same way at each end of next and foll 4th row. 37 sts. Beg with a p row, work 17 rows in st st, ending with a p row.

Next row: Cast on 61 sts, k to end. Now join work to cont in rounds, making sure sts are not twisted when joining and inserting marker to denote beg of rounds. K 1 round.

Next round: (eyelets) K4, (yfwd, k2tog, k8) twice, yfwd, k2tog, k10, (yfwd, k2tog, k8) twice, yfwd, k2tog, k40.

Cont in rounds of st st (every round k) until work measures 24cm (9½in) from cast-on sts before eyelets, ending at marker.

Next round: K2tog, k8, sl 1, k1, psso, place marker, k2tog, k33, sl 1, k1, psso, place marker, k2tog, k8, sl 1, k1, psso, place marker, k2tog, k33, sl 1, k1, psso.

Next round: K2tog, k to 2 sts before marker, (sl 1, k1, psso, k2tog, k to 2 sts before next marker) three times, sl 1, k1, psso.

Rep last round until 2 sts rem between markers at sides. 58 sts. Graft rem sts of back and front tog to close bottom of bag.

LONG STRAP:

With 4mm (no. 8/US 6) needles cast on 7 sts.

Cont in rib as foll:

1st row: (RS) K1, (p1, k1) to end.

2nd row: P1, (k1, p1) to end.

Rep these 2 rows until strap measures 80cm (32in).

Cast/bind off in rib.

SHORT STRAP: (Make 2)

With 4mm (no. 8/US 6) needles cast on 7 sts. Work 8cm (3in) in rib as given for Long strap. Cast/bind off in rib.

PURSE:

With 4mm (no. 8/US 6) needles cast on 2 sts.

1st row: (RS) K2, inc in both sts. 4 sts.

2nd row: P to end.

3rd row: Inc in first st, k to last st, inc in last st. 6 sts.

4th row: P to end.

Rep 3rd and 4th rows 8 times more. 22 sts. Cont in st st until Purse measures 16cm (6¼in) from end of shaped section, ending with a p row. Cast/bind off.

 ## Making up

Fold long strap in half to find centre point. Place strap vertically on centre back of bag, with centre point in line with top edge of front. Attach at this point with a line of backstitch across strap. Folding strap down, spread two ends slightly apart, one on top of the other. Reinforce with a line of backstitch across straps, through all layers, 3cm (1¼in) down from top. Thread adjustable buckle pieces on to strap ends. Thread short straps through fixed buckle pieces so they are folded in half. Sew in position on bag back with outer lower corner of strap at top of shapings for bag bottom. Reinforce by working a square of backstitch through all 3 layers. Close buckles and adjust strap lengths.

Make two 55cm (22in) twisted cords and another one 25cm (10in) in length. Thread two longer cords in and out of eyelet holes around top edge of bag and coming through to right side at centre front. Sew fixed ends in place at edge of flap on WS at either side and tie free ends, gathering top edge of bag. Sew larger button and press stud (popper snap) to flap with under half of press stud (popper snap) 8cm (3in) down from top edge of bag centre front.

To complete purse, fold lower straight section in half, with RS facing, so that cast/bound-off edge is level with end of flap shaping. Join side seams and turn to RS. Sew button and press stud (popper snap) in place on flap. Attach one end of remaining cord to purse and other end to bag on WS at one side seam.

Heirloom baby bootees

Small but perfectly formed, these tiny bootees will be treasured long after they are outgrown.

Irresistibly cute and worked in easy moss/seed stitch and stocking/stockinette stitch, you could make these tiny shoes for a boy or girl by changing the colours of the embroidery.

GETTING STARTED

Even a new knitter can cope with the shaping involved in making bootees

Size:

To fit baby 0–6 months; sole is 9cm (3½in) long

How much yarn:

1 x 50g (2oz) ball of Debbie Bliss Baby Cashmerino, approx 125m (137 yards) per ball

Needles:

Pair of 3.25mm (no. 10/US 3) knitting needles

Additional items:

Scraps of yarn in two different shades of contrasting colour A and B

2 small shank buttons

Safety pins/holders

Tension/gauge:

25 sts and 34 rows measure 10cm (4in) square over st st on 3.25mm (no. 10/US 3) needles

IT IS ESSENTIAL TO WORK TO THE STATED TENSION/ GAUGE TO ACHIEVE SUCCESS

What you have to do:

Work strap and around top of bootee in moss/seed stitch. Work main fabric in stocking/stockinette stitch. Work top of foot, then pick up stitches for side of foot. Use simple shaping for sole. Embroider loop stitch edging around top of foot and rose on front of foot.

The Yarn

Debbie Bliss Baby Cashmerino is a luxurious blend of 55% merino wool, 33% microfibre and 12% cashmere in a 4-ply (fingering) weight. It is beautifully soft for a baby and can be machine washed at a low temperature. There are also plenty of fabulous shades to choose from.

Instructions

Abbreviations:

cm = centimetre(s); **foll** = follows;
k = knit; **p** = purl; **rem** = remaining;
rep = repeat; **RS** = right side;
st(s) = stitch(es); **st st** = stocking/
stockinette stitch; **tog** = together;
yfwd = yarn forward/yarn over

RIGHT BOOTEE:

Cast on 9 sts.

1st row: P1, *k1, p1, rep from * to end.
Rep this row to form moss/seed st.
Work 2 more rows. Cut off yarn and leave
sts on a safety pin. Cast on 26 sts.

1st row: (RS) *P1, k1, rep from * to end.

2nd row: K1, *p1, k1, rep from * to last 5
sts, yfwd, k2tog, p1, k1, p1.

3rd row: As 1st row.

4th row: K1, *p1, k1, rep from * 3 times
more, cast/bind off rem 17 sts.
Turn work, rejoin yarn to inner edge of
9 sts on needle and cast on 18 sts, turn and
work in moss/seed st across 9 sts on
safety pin. 36 sts. Work 4 rows in moss/
seed sts across all 36 sts.

Next row: K23, turn.

Next row: P10, turn.

** Working on these 10 sts only, work
6 rows in st st. Cut off yarn and leave sts on
needle.

With RS of work facing and using needle
holding 13 sts, rejoin yarn at division of
instep and pick up and k7 sts along one side
of foot, k across 10 sts on needle, pick up
and k7 sts along other side of foot and k
across 13 sts on other needle. 50 sts.
Beg with a p row, work 7 rows in st st. Cont
in reverse st st as foll:

Shape sole:

1st row: P to end.

2nd row: *K1, k2tog, k19, k2tog, k1, rep
from * once more. 46 sts.

3rd row: P to end.

4th row: *K1, k2tog, k17, k2tog, k1, rep
from * once more. 42 sts.

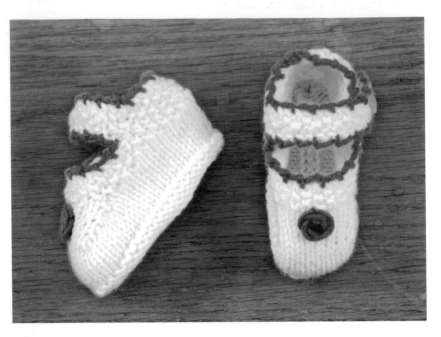

5th row: P to end.
6th row: *K1, k2tog, k15, k2tog, k1, rep from *
once more. 38 sts. Cast/bind off purlwise.

LEFT BOOTEE:
Cast on 26 sts.
1st row: (RS) *K1, p1, rep from * to end.
2nd row: (P1, k1) twice, yfwd, k2tog, *p1, k1, rep
from * to end.
3rd row: As 1st row.
4th row: Cast/bind off 17 sts, cut off yarn and
sl rem 9 sts on to a safety pin.
Cast on 9 sts.
1st row: P1, *k1, p1, rep from * to end.
Rep this row to form moss/seed st. Work 2 more
rows.
Next row: P1, (k1, p1) 4 times, turn and cast on
18 sts, turn and commence at inner edge, work in
moss/seed st across 9 sts on safety pin.
36 sts. Work 4 rows in moss/seed sts across all 36 sts.
Next row: K23, turn.
Next row: P10, turn.
Complete as given for Right bootee from
** to end.

 Making up

Fold cast/bound-off edge in half and join using a
flat stitch. Join row ends to form back of foot.
Embroidery:
Embroider loop stitch edging around top edge
of bootee and strap in A as foll: insert needle
downwards through loop of working thread and
edge of fabric, bringing it out again over thread.
Work into alternate knitted sts. Embroider a rose
on centre of foot as foll: with B, make a 5-pointed
star about 1.5cm (½in) in diameter, then weave
yarn under and over the arms of the star to form
a complete circle. Change to A and continue
weaving the yarn through the arms of the star
until it resembles a rose and the arms are no
longer visible.
Fold over straps and secure at sides by stitching
on buttons. Fill bootees with tissue paper to form
foot shape. Steam and allow to dry.

Baseball-style hooded top

A plain body and striped sleeves give this classic hooded top a distinctly sporty look.

This sports-style sweater with a hood and large front pocket will be popular with both girls and boys. The easy drop-shoulder style is knitted in simple stocking/stockinette stitch, while the sleeves are striped in a contrast colour.

GETTING STARTED

Simple drop-shoulder style with minimum of shaping but pay attention to working front pocket section

Size:

To fit chest: 61[66:71:76]cm/24[26:28:30]in

Actual size: 73[78:84:89]cm/28¾[30¾:33:35]in

Length: 36[40:44:48]cm/14[15¾:17½:19]in

Sleeve seam: 28[31:34:37]cm/11[12¼:13½:14½]in

Note: *Figures in square brackets [ ] refer to larger sizes; where there is only one set of figures, it applies to all sizes*

How much yarn:

7[7:8:8] x 50g (2oz) balls of Rowan 100% pure wool DK, approx 130m (142 yards) per ball in main colour M

1[2:2:2] balls in contrast colour C

Needles:

Pair of 3.25mm (no. 10/US 3) knitting needles

Pair of 4mm (no. 8/US 6) knitting needles

Additional items:

Stitch holder, Spare needle

Tension/gauge:

22 sts and 30 rows measure 10cm (4in) square over st st on 4mm (no. 8/US 6) needles

IT IS ESSENTIAL TO WORK TO THE STATED TENSION/GAUGE TO ACHIEVE SUCCESS

What you have to do:

Work double (k2, p2) rib for edgings. Work main fabric in stocking/stockinette stitch. Knit pocket lining separately, then join in leaving front pocket stitches on a holder. Knit front pocket stitches separately, then join to main fabric by working together with stitches of main fabric. Make two-colour stripe pattern for sleeves, carrying yarns up side of work.

The Yarn

Rowan 100% Pure Wool DK is a double knitting (light worsted) weight. A slight twist to the fibres helps to produce good-looking stocking/stockinette stitch fabrics. The colour range is comprehensive with plenty of choice for working stripes and colour patterns.

Abbreviations:

alt = alternate;
beg = beginning;
cm = centimetre(s);
cont = continue;
dec = decrease(ing);
foll = following;
inc = increase(ing);
k = knit;
m1 = make one stitch by picking up horizontal strand lying between needles and working into back of it;
p = purl; **patt** = pattern;
psso = pass slipped stitch over;
rem = remaining;
rep = repeat;
RS = right side;
sl = slip; **st(s)** = stitch(es);
st st = stocking/stockinette stitch;
tog = together;
WS = wrong side

Instructions

BACK:

With 3.25mm (no. 10/US 3) needles and M, cast on 74[78:86:90] sts.
1st row: (RS) K2, (p2, k2) to end.
2nd row: P2, (k2, p2) to end.
Rib 4[4:6:6] rows more as set.
Change to 4mm (no. 8/US 6) needles.
Inc row: (RS) K2[3:8:9], *m1, k10[8:10:8], rep from * to last 2[3:8:9] sts, m1, k to end. 82[88:94:100] sts. **
Beg with a p row, cont in st st until work measures 36[40:44:48] cm/14[15¾:17½:19]in from cast-on edge, ending witha p row.

Shape shoulders:

Cast/bind off 9[10:10:11] sts at beg of next 4 rows and 9[9:11:11] sts at beg of foll 2 rows. Cast/bind off loosely rem 28[30:32:34] sts.

POCKET LINING:

With 4mm (no. 8/US 6) needles and M, cast on 44[46:50:52] sts. Beg with a k row, work 14[18:22:26] rows in st st, ending with a p row. Cut off yarn and leave sts on a holder.

FRONT:

Work as given for Back to **. Beg with a p row, work 13[17:21:25] rows in st st, ending with a p row.

Place pocket:

Next row: (RS) K19[21:22:24], sl next 44[46:50:52] sts on to a holder, then with RS facing k across 44[46:50:52] lining sts, k rem 19[21:22:24] sts. 82[88:94:100] sts. Beg with a p row, work 23[25:27:29] rows more in st st, ending with a p row.
Cut off yarn and leave sts on a spare needle.
With RS facing, rejoin yarn to 44[46:50:52] front pocket sts and beg with a k row, work 24[26:28:30] rows in st st, ending with a p row. Cut off yarn.
Next row: With RS facing, return to 82[88:94:100] sts on spare needle, join in yarn and k19[21:22:24], fold up 44[46:50:52] front pocket sts and, holding both needles with pocket sts tog in left hand and points tog, k next 44[46:50:52] sts through both pieces tog, taking 1 st from front pocket tog with 1 st from back pocket for each st, k rem 19 [21:22:24] sts. 82[88:94:100] sts.

Beg with a p row, cont in st st until work measures 8[10:12:14] rows less than Back to shoulder, ending with a p row.

Shape neck:

Next row: (RS) K33[36:39:42], cast/bind off loosely next 16 sts, k to end. Cont on last set of 33[36:39:42] sts for right front neck as foll:

Dec 1 st at neck edge on next 6[7:8:9] rows. 27[29:31:33] sts. Work 2[3:4:5] rows straight, ending at shoulder edge.

Shape shoulder:

Cast/bind off 9[10:10:11] sts at beg of next and foll alt row. Work 1 row. Cast/bind off rem 9[9:11:11] sts.

With WS facing, rejoin yarn at neck edge to rem 33[36:39:42] sts and work to match first side, reversing shaping and working 1 row less before shaping shoulder.

SLEEVES: (Make 2)

With 3.25mm (no.10/US 3) needles and M, cast on 42[46:50:54] sts. Work 6[6:8:8] rows in rib as given for Back.

Change to 4mm (no. 8/US 6) needles. Beg with a k row, cont in st st and stripe patt of 2 rows C, 2 rows M throughout, AT SAME TIME inc 1 st at each end of next row and every foll 4th row to 74[74:78:78] sts, then at each end of every foll 6th row to 78[84:90:96] sts. Work 5 rows straight. Cast/bind off with same colour as last stripe.

HOOD:

With 3.25mm (no. 10/US 3) needles and M, cast on 134[138:142:146] sts. Work 4 rows in rib as given for Back. Change to 4mm (no. 8/US 6) needles. Beg with a k row, work 12 rows in st st.

Shape hood:

Next row: (RS) K1, sl 1, k1, psso, k to last 3 sts, k2tog, k1. Work 3 rows straight. Rep last 4 rows 5[5:6:6] times more. 122[126:128:132] sts.

Next row: K1, sl 1, k1, psso, k56[58:59:61], sl 1, k1, psso, k2tog, k56[58:59:61], k2tog, k1.

Next row: P to end.

Next row: K57[59:60:62], sl 1, k1, psso, k2tog, 57[59:60:62].

Next row: P to end.

Cont in this way, dec 2 sts at centre on next row and every alt row, AT SAME TIME dec 1 st at each end on next and every foll 4th row until 98[102:104:108] sts rem.

Next row: (WS) P49[51:52:54], turn and sl these sts just worked on to a spare needle, p rem 49[51:52:54] sts. Now with the two needles holding sts in left hand, RS of work tog and WS facing, taking one st from each piece and working them tog, cast/bind off all sts.

POCKET EDGINGS:

With 3.25mm (no. 8/US 6) needle, M and RS of work facing, pick up and k22[26:26:30] sts along one pocket opening. Beg with 2nd row, rib 3 rows as given for Back. Cast/bind off in rib.

Work other side to match.

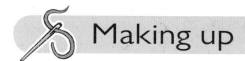

Making up

Press, following instructions on ball band. Join shoulder seams. Sew in sleeves to approximately 18[19:21:22]cm/ 7[7½:8:8½]in below shoulders. Join side and sleeve seams. Catch down pocket lining and pocket edgings. Sew shaped edges of hood to neck edge, placing beg and end of cast-on row meeting at centre front neck and base of hood cast/ bound-off edge to centre back neck.

Driving in my car

This soft but durable toy makes the perfect gift for a car-mad toddler.

A fabulous nursery toy or just a cute ornament for your shelves, this toy-town car is knitted in stocking/ stockinette stitch and has separate wheels that are stitched in place.

The Yarn

Patons Diploma Gold DK is a practical combination of 55% wool, 25% acrylic and 20% nylon. It can be machine washed – essential for toys – and there are plenty of shades to choose your own colour schemes.

GETTING STARTED

 Stitches involved are not difficult but intarsia techniques need practise and careful assembly is essential

Size:

Car is approximately 15cm high x 20cm long (6in x 8in)

How much yarn:

1 x 50g (2oz) ball of Patons Diploma Gold DK, approx 120m (131 yards) per ball, in each of four colours A, B, C and D

Oddment of yarn in colour E

Needles:

Pair of 4mm (no. 8/US 6) knitting needles

Additional items:

Washable polyester toy filling

Tension/gauge:

22 sts and 28 rows measure 10cm (4in) square over st st on 4mm (no. 8/US 6) needles

IT IS ESSENTIAL TO WORK TO THE STATED TENSION/GAUGE TO ACHIEVE SUCCESS

What you have to do:

Work car sides and centre panel in three separate pieces, following charts. Use intarsia techniques with small separate balls of yarn for knitting in windows. Outline window edges in embroidered backstitch. Make circular wheels using turning rows and strips in garter stitch. Make separate bobbles for tyre centres and headlamps. Stuff sections with toy filling, stitch on wheels.

Abbreviations:

beg = beginning;
cm = centimetre(s);
cont = continue;
dec = decreasing;
inc = make one stitch by knitting into front and back of stitch;
k = knit;
p = purl; **patt** = pattern;
rem = remaining;
rep = repeat;
RS = right side;
st st = stocking/stockinette stitch); **st(s)** = stitch(es);
WS = wrong side;
tbl = through back of loops;
tog = together;
yrn = wrap yarn around right-hand needle from back to front/yarn over

Note: When working windows, use a separate small ball of yarn for each area of colour and twist yarns tog on WS of work when changing colour to avoid holes forming.

Instructions

CAR:
Right side:
With A, cast on 44 sts. Beg with a k row, cont in st st and work in patt from Chart 1, dec as indicated. After 42 rows have been completed, cast/bind off.

Left side:
With A, cast on 44 sts. Beg with a k row, cont in st st and work in patt from Chart 2, dec as indicated. After 42 rows have been completed, cast/bind off.

Centre panel:
With A, cast on 17 sts. Beg with a k row, cont in st st and work 27 rows.
Next row: (WS) K to end to form foldline. Beg with a k row, cont in st st and work 22 rows, ending with a p row.

Front windscreen/windshield:
*Next row: (RS) K3 A, 11 B, 3 A.
Next row: P3 A, 11 B, 3 A.*
Rep last 2 rows 6 times more.
Next row: K4 A, 9 B, 4 A.
Next row: P5 A, 7 B, 5 A.** Using A only cont in st st for a further 22 rows.

Rear window:
Next row: K5 A, 7 B, 5 A.
Next row: P4 A, 9 B, 4 A.

Rep from * to * as given for Front windscreen/windshield twice, then work as given for Front windscreen/windshield from ** to **.
With A only cont in st st for a further 21 rows.
Next row: (WS) K to end to form foldline.
Beg with a k row, cont in st st and work 28 rows, ending with a p row. Cast/bind off.

Wheels:
Outer circles: (Make 8 alike)
With D, cast on 5 sts.
1st row: (RS) K5.
2nd row: K4, turn.
3rd row: Yrn, k4.
4th row: K3, turn.
5th row: Yrn, k3.
6th row: K2, turn.
7th row: Yrn, k2.
8th row: K2, (k2tog tbl) 3 times. 5 sts.
Rep last 8 rows 7 times more. Cast/bind off. Thread the yarn through sts at the centre of circle and pull up, now join cast/bound-off and cast on-edges.

Tyres: (Make 4)
With 4mm (no. 8) needles and D, cast on 40 sts. K 6 rows. Cast/bind off.

Bobbles: (Make 6–4 for centre of tyres and 2 for front headlamps)
With C, cast on 3 sts.
Next row: Inc in each st to end. 6 sts. Beg with a p row, work 5 rows st st, ending with a p row.
Next row: (K2tog) 3 times. 3 sts.
Cut off yarn, leaving a long end. Thread yarn through rem 3 sts, then thread yarn around outer edges of bobble and pull up securely.

Chart 1

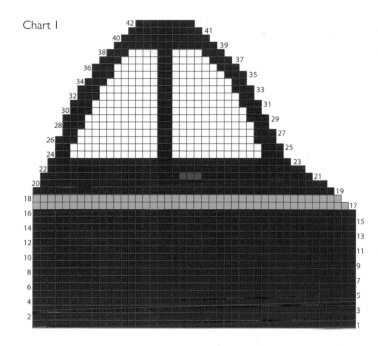

Chart 2

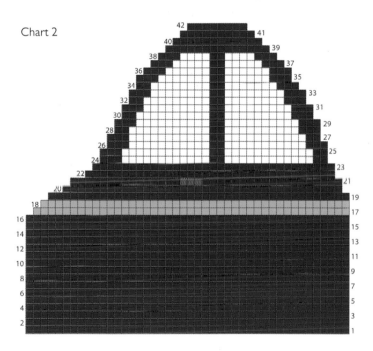

 Making up

With E, work backstitch around the outer edges of windows on left and right sides and also on centre panel. Swiss darn door handles on sides as marked. Join cast-on and cast/bound-off edges of car centre panel to form a circle and place this seam at centre of cast-on edge of right front. With ridge rows matching front and back corners of right front, sew centre panel in place around outer edges. Sew centre panel to left front in the same way, but leaving a gap in seam at cast-on edge. Stuff car and then slip stitch gap in seam to close it.

Join row ends of tyres to form a circle. Make up wheels by sewing centre in place between two outer circles, leaving a small gap in one seam. Stuff firmly and close gap in the seam.

Place wheels on sides of car with half extending below lower edge and sew securely in place. Sew one bobble in centre of each wheel, then pass needle through centre of car to opposite wheel and pull gently to create a 'dimple' in centre of wheel. Sew securely in place behind bobbles.

Sew two more bobbles to front of car level with stripe on sides to form headlamps.

Baby crossover cardigan

Spoil your baby with this beautiful classic cardigan knitted in the softest yarn.

Worked in a luxurious baby yarn, with pretty shaded spots, this is the perfect cardigan for a special small person.

GETTING STARTED

 Simple fabric and shaping but working Fair Isle pattern requires concentration

Size:

To fit age: 3–6[6–9:9–12] months

To fit chest: 46[48:51]cm/18[19:20]in

Length: 19[20:22]cm/7½[8:8¾]in

Sleeve seam: 14.5[15.5:16.5]cm5¾[6:6½]in

Note: Figures in square brackets [ ] refer to larger sizes; where there is only one set of figures, it applies to all sizes

How much yarn:

3[3:3] x 50g (2oz) balls of Sublime Baby Cashmere Merino Silk DK, approx 116m (127 yards) per ball, in main colour A

1 ball in each of three contrast colours B, C and D

Needles:

Pair of 3.25mm (no. 10/US 3) knitting needles

Pair of 4mm (no. 8/US 6) knitting needles

Additional items:

3.5mm (UK 9/US 4/E) crochet hook

6 small buttons

Tension/gauge:

22 sts and 28 rows measure 10cm (4in) square over st st on 4mm (no. 8/US 6) needles

IT IS ESSENTIAL TO WORK TO THE STATED TENSION/ GAUGE TO ACHIEVE SUCCESS

What you have to do:

Work lower hems in garter stitch (every row knit). Work main fabric in stocking/stockinette stitch with Fair Isle spot pattern, stranding yarn not in use across back of work. Change colour of spots every 12 rows. Use simple shaping for armholes, front slopes and sleeves. Pick up stitches around neckline and work garter stitch band. Crochet button loops at side edges of fronts.

The Yarn

Sublime Baby Cashmere Merino Silk DK is a blend of 75% merino wool, 20% silk and 5% cashmere. It is soft and smooth for a baby's skin and there is a small palette of adorable baby shades to choose from.

Abbreviations:

alt = alternate;
beg = beginning;
ch = chain;
cm = centimetre(s);
cont = continue;
dc = double crochet (US
sc = single crochet);
dec = decrease(ing);
foll = follow(s)(ing);
g st = garter stitch (every
row knit);
inc = increase(ing);
k = knit; **p** = purl;
patt = pattern;
rem = remain(ing);
rep = repeat;
RS = right side;
ss = slip stitch (crochet);
st(s) = stitch(es);
st st = stocking/
stockinette stitch;
tog = together;
WS = wrong side

Instructions

BACK:

With 3.25mm (no. 10/US 3) needles and A, cast on 58[62:66] sts. *K 3 rows. Change to 4mm (no. 8/US 6) needles. Beg with a k row, work 2 rows in st st. Join in B. Stranding yarn not in use loosely across WS of work, cont in Fair Isle patt as foll:

1st row: (RS) K1[3:1] A, (1 B, 3 A) to last 1[3:5] sts, 1 B, 0[2:4] A.

2nd row: With A, p to end.

3rd row: With A, k to end.

4th row: P2[0:2] A, (1 B, 3 A) to last 0[2:4] sts, 1 B, 0[1:3] A.

5th row: With A, k to end.

6th row: With A, p to end. These 6 rows form patt. * Rep them once more using B as contrast colour. Cont in colour sequence of 12 rows each of C, D and B as contrast colours, patt 10[12:18] rows more, so ending with a WS row.

Shape armholes:

Keeping patt correct as set, cast/bind off 4 sts at beg of next 2 rows. 50[54:58] sts. Patt 24[26:26] rows straight, so ending with a WS row.

Shape back neck and shoulders:

Keeping patt correct as set, cast/bind off 5[5:6] sts at beg of next 2 rows.

Next row: Cast/bind off 5[5:6] sts, k until there are 7[8:8] sts on right-hand needle,

turn and complete this side of neck first.

Next row: P2tog, p to end.
Cast/bind off rem 6[7:7] sts.
With RS of work facing, rejoin yarn to rem sts and cast/bind off centre 16[18:18] sts, k to end.

Next row: Cast/bind off 5[5:6] sts, p to last 2 sts, p2tog.
Work 1 row. Cast/bind off rem 6[7:7] sts.

RIGHT FRONT:

With 3.25mm (no. 10/US 3) needles and A, cast on 58[62:66] sts. Work as given for Back from * to *. Cont in patt and stripe sequence as given for Back, patt 4[6:8] more rows, so ending with a WS row (for Left Front, work 3[5:7] rows here, so ending with a RS row).

Shape front slope:

Keeping patt correct, cast/bind off at beg of next and foll alt rows 4 sts twice, 3[3:4] sts once and 0[3:3] sts once. 47[48:51] sts. Now dec 1 st at front slope on every row until 39[42:41] sts rem, ending with a RS row (for Left front, end with a WS row here).

Shape armhole:

Next row: Cast/bind off 4 sts, patt to last 2 sts, work 2 tog. 34[37:36] sts. Keeping armhole edge straight, cont to dec at front slope only on every row until 18[19:21] sts rem, then on foll 2 alt rows.

16[17:19] sts. Work 5[5:8] rows straight, so ending at armhole edge.

Shape shoulder:
Cast/bind off 5[5:6] sts at beg of next and foll alt row. Work 1 row. Cast/bind off rem 6[7:7] sts.

LEFT FRONT:
Work as given for Right front, noting the bracketed exceptions.

SLEEVES: (Make 2)
With 3.25mm (no. 10/US 3) needles and A, cast on 34[36:38] sts. K 3 rows. Change to 4mm (no. 8/US 6) needles. Beg with a k row, work 2 rows in st st. Join in B. Cont in Fair Isle patt and shape as foll:

1st row: (RS) Inc in first st, k0[1:2] A, (1 B, 3 A) to last 1[2:3] sts, 0[1:1] B, 0[0:1] A, inc in last st.

2nd row: With A, p to end.

3rd row: With A, k to end.

4th row: P3[4:1] A, (1 B, 3 A) to last 1[2:3] sts, 1 A[1 B:1 B], 0[1:2] A.

5th row: With A, k to end.

6th row: With A, p to end.

Cont in patt as set and colour sequence as given for Back, inc 1 st at each end of next and every foll 6th row until there are 48[50:52] sts, working extra sts into patt. Work 3[5:9] rows straight, so ending with a WS row. Cast/bind off.

FRONT SLOPE AND NECKBAND:
Join shoulder seams.

With 3.25mm (no. 10/US 3) needles, A and RS of work facing, beg at cast/bound-off sts of front slope and pick up and PURL 46[48:54] sts evenly up shaped edge of Right front to shoulder, 20[22:22] sts around back neck and 46[48:54] sts down shaped edge of Left front to beg of shaping. 112[118:130] sts. K 3 rows. Cast/bind off loosely.

Right front button loops:
With 3.5mm (UK 9/US 4/E) crochet hook, A and RS of front facing sideways on, work 2dc (US sc) into edge of g st hem, (6ch, ss into last dc (US sc) worked, 1dc (US sc) into each of next 6[7:8] row ends) twice, 6ch, ss into last dc (US sc) worked, 2dc (US sc) into edge of g st band. Fasten off.

Left front button loops:
With 3.5mm (UK 9/US 4/E) crochet hook, A and RS of front facing sideways on, work 2dc (US sc) into edge

of g st band, (6ch, ss into last dc (US sc) worked, 1dc (US sc) into each of next 6[7:8] row ends) twice, 6ch, ss into last dc (US sc) worked, 2dc into edge of g st hem. Fasten off.

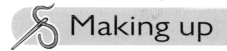

Making up

Sew in sleeves, joining final rows of sleeve to cast/bound-off sts at underarm. Join side and sleeve seams.

For a girl:
Wrap Right front over Left front. Sew 3 buttons to inside side seam to correspond with button loops on edge of Left front and 3 buttons to outside seam to correspond with button loops on edge of Right front.

For a boy:
Wrap Left front over Right front. Sew 3 buttons to inside side seam to correspond with button loops on edge of Right front and 3 buttons to outside seam to correspond with button loops on edge of Left front.

Nursery wall hanging

Work patchwork squares in bright colours and add some appliqué for a stunning design.

A mix of antique charm and contemporary colours, this wall hanging with its knitted-in motifs and sewn-on appliqué shapes is perfect for hanging in a nursery

The Yarn

Debbie Bliss Rialto DK contains 100% merino wool. Its smooth construction gives good stitch definition for stocking/stockinette stitch fabrics and there is an excellent shade range for exciting colour work.

GETTING STARTED

Easy stocking/stockinette stitch fabric but colour motifs need intarsia skills and neat sewing is required for a successful finish

Size:

Hanging is approximately 34cm x 47cm (13½in x 18½in), including loops

How much yarn:

1 x 50g (2oz) ball of Debbie Bliss Rialto DK, approx 105m (115 yards) per ball, in each of seven colours A, B, C, D, E, F and G

Needles:

Pair of 3.75mm (no. 9/US 5) knitting needles

Additional items:

32cm x 43cm (12½in x 17in) piece of lightweight polyester wadding/batting

37cm x 46cm (14½in x 18in) piece of red cotton fabric for backing

13cm (5in) square of spotted or plain cotton fabric in purple

13cm x 7cm (5in x 2¾in) piece of spotted or plain cotton fabric in red

Scrap of iron-on interfacing

Purple and red sewing threads

Tension/gauge:

24 sts and 30 rows measure 10cm (4in) square over st st on 3.75mm (no. 9/US 5) needles

IT IS ESSENTIAL TO WORK TO THE STATED TENSION/ GAUGE TO ACHIEVE SUCCESS

What you have to do:

Work three vertical strips of four squares each in stocking/stockinette stitch, following charts for patterns. Use intarsia or Fair Isle techniques of stranding yarns as appropriate. Swiss darn on smaller motifs and sew on fabric appliqué shapes. Pick up stitches around edges for borders and hanging loops. Follow instructions to add wadding/batting and sew on fabric backing.

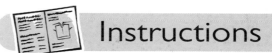 ## Instructions

WALL HANGING

Right-hand strip:

With C, cast on 27 sts.

Beg with a k row, cont in st st and patt from Chart 1 until 33rd row is complete. Cont in st st, work 33 rows from each of Charts 2, 3 and 4. Cast/bind off.

Centre strip:

With A, cast on 27 sts.

Beg with a k row, work 33 rows in st st. Cut off A and cont in E. Beg with a p row, work 33 rows in st st. Cut off E and join in A. Cont in patt from Chart 7, omitting small heart motif (this can be Swiss darned on later after strip is complete). Cut off A and join in C. Cont in patt from Chart 8 until 33rd row is complete. Cast/ bind off.

Foll Charts 5 and 6 to Swiss darn motifs on to plain

Abbreviations:

beg = beginning;
cm = centimetre(s);
cont = continue;
foll = following; **k** = knit;
p = purl; **patt** = pattern;
rem = remaining;
rep = repeat;
RS = right side;
st(s) = stitch(es);
st st = stocking/
stockinette stitch;
tog = together;
WS = wrong side

Notes:

When working in patt from Charts 1, 3, 5, 7, 9 and 11, read odd-numbered (RS) rows from right to left and even-numbered (WS) rows from left to right. Reverse this process for charts 2, 4, 6, 8, 10 and 12. Use separate small balls of yarn for each area of colour and twist yarns tog on WS of work when changing colours to avoid holes forming. Where two colours are used in a small area, it may be possible to strand or weave in yarn across WS of work.

squares in E and A. Complete Chart 7 if required.

Left-hand strip:

With D, cast on 27 sts. Beg with a k row, cont in st st and work 33 rows from each of Charts 9 and 10. Join in F. Beg with a k row, work 33 rows in st st. Cut off F and join in A. Work 33 rows in patt from Chart 12. Cast/bind off.
Foll Chart 11 to Swiss darn motif on to plain square in F.

Side borders:

Join three strips, carefully matching colour change at each square.
With B and RS of work facing, pick up and k 104 sts along one side edge (26 sts from each square). K 3 rows. Cast/bind off.
Rep along other side edge.

Lower border:

With B and RS of work facing, pick up and k 83 sts along lower edge. K 3 rows. Cast/bind off.

Hanging loops:

With B and RS of work facing, pick up and k 83 sts along upper edge. K 3 rows.
Next row: (RS) K11, turn and cont on these sts only.
K 35 rows. Cast/bind off.
*Return to rem sts and, with RS facing, rejoin yarn to next st.

Next row: (RS) Cast/bind off 13 sts, k until there are 11 sts on right-hand needle, turn and cont on these sts only. K 35 rows. Cast/bind off.*
Rep from * to * once more.
Next row: (RS) Cast off 13 sts, k to end. 11 sts. K 35 rows. Cast/bind off.
Fold each loop in half to WS and slip stitch in place level with first row of loop.

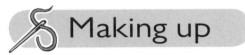

Making up

Press carefully according to directions on ball band.
Apply iron-on interfacing to WS of purple and red spotted or plain cotton fabric. Using templates, cut 'A' from purple fabric and '1' from red fabric. Using photograph (above left) as a guide, tack/baste appliqué shapes in place on knitted background. Sew in place with small blanket stitches.
Place lightweight polyester wadding/batting on WS of hanging and tack/baste in place around outer edges, trimming to size if necessary. Turn outer edges of red backing fabric to WS so that backing is same size as knitted piece. Tack/baste in place on back of hanging over polyester wadding/batting, then oversew around outer edges using matching sewing thread. Using red sewing thread, work a row of running stitch along vertical and horizontal lines between each square, avoiding appliqué shapes.

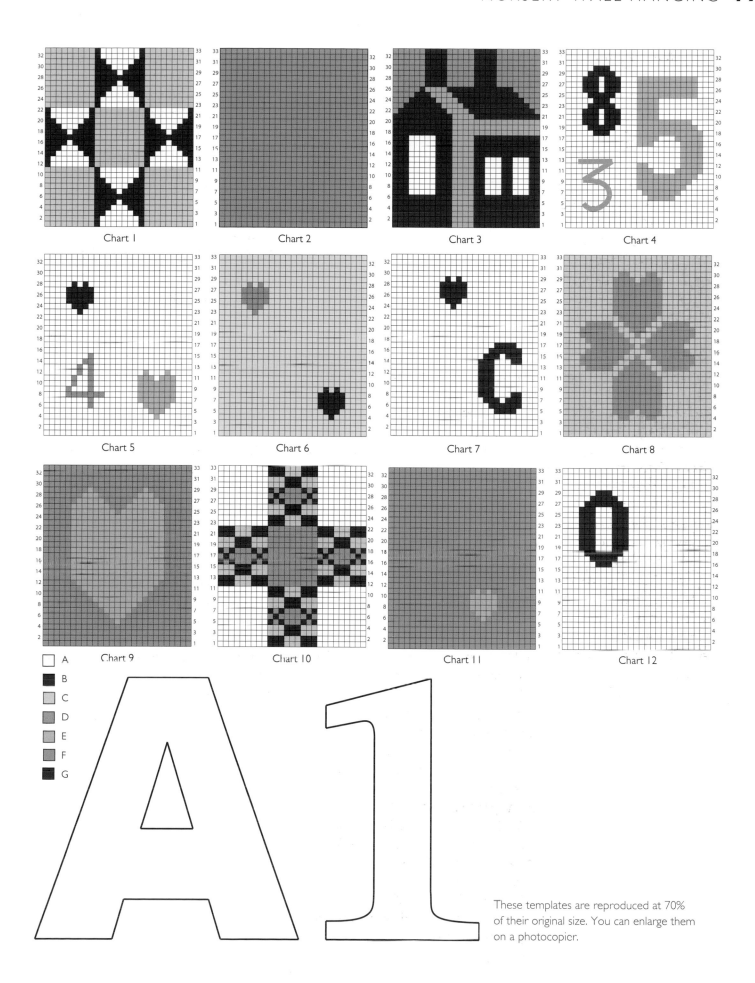

Chart 1

Chart 2

Chart 3

Chart 4

Chart 5

Chart 6

Chart 7

Chart 8

Chart 9

Chart 10

Chart 11

Chart 12

A
B
C
D
E
F
G

These templates are reproduced at 70% of their original size. You can enlarge them on a photocopier.

Child's Aran sweater

Practise your cabling skills with this miniature version of a popular classic.

Richly embossed Aran (fisherman) patterns look striking in this drop-shoulder sweater with a funnel neckline.

GETTING STARTED

 Establishing and working Aran patterns is a challenge and there is neck shaping to contend with

Size:

To fit chest: 56[61:66]cm/22[24:26]in
Actual size: 59[65:71]cm/23½[25½:28]in
Length: 38[41:44]cm/15[16:17½]in
Sleeve seam: 26[29:32]cm/10¼[11½:12½]in
Note: *Figures in square brackets [ ] refer to larger sizes; where there is only one set of figures, it applies to all sizes*

How much yarn:

7[8:8] x 50g (2oz) balls of Debbie Bliss Cashmerino Aran, approx 90m (98 yards) per ball

Needles:

Pair of 4mm (no. 8/US 6) knitting needles
Pair of 5mm (no. 6/US 8) knitting needles
Cable needle

Tension/gauge:

25 sts and 26 rows measure 10cm (4in) square over blackberry st on 5mm (no. 6/US 8) needles
IT IS ESSENTIAL TO WORK TO THE STATED TENSION/ GAUGE TO ACHIEVE SUCCESS

What you have to do:

Work throughout in panels of blackberry stitch and cables. Use simple shaping for front neck and sleeves. Pick up stitches around neckline and work neckband in double (knit two, purl two) rib.

The Yarn

Debbie Bliss Cashmerino Aran is a blend of 55% merino wool, 33% microfibre and 12% cashmere. It is luxuriously soft and warm for a child and it can be machine washed at a low temperature. There are plenty of fabulous colours to choose from.

 # Instructions

BACK:

With 5mm (no. 6/US 8) needles cast on 78[86:94] sts.
Foundation row: (WS) K2, p4, k1, (p3tog, (k1, p1, k1) all in next st) 1[1:2] times, k1, p2, *k3, p4, k3, p2, k1, (p3tog, (k1, p1, k1) all in next st) 1[2:2] times, k1, p2, k2, p6, k2, p2, k1, ((k1, p1, k1) all in next st, p3tog) 1[2:2] times, k1, p2, k3, p4, k3*, p2, k1, ((k1, p1, k1) all in next st, p3tog) 1[1:2] times, k1, p4, k2.
Cont in patt as foll:
1st row: (RS) P2, k4, p6[6:10], Tw2, *p3, C4B, p3, Tw2, p6[10:10], Tw2, p2, C6B, p2, Tw2, p6[10:10], Tw2, p3, C4B, p3* , Tw2, p6[6:10], k4, p2.
2nd row: K2, p4, k1, ((k1, p1, k1) all in next st, p3tog) 1[1:2] times, k1, p2, *k3, p4, k3, p2, k1, ((k1, p1, k1) all in next st, p3tog) 1[2:2] times, k1, p2, k2, p6, k2, p2, k1, (p3tog, (k1, p1, k1) all in next st) 1[2:2] times, k1, p2, k3, p4, k3 *, p2, k1, (p3tog, (k1, p1, k1) all in next st] 1[1:2] times, k1, p4, k2.

Abbreviations:

beg = beginning;
cm = centimetre(s);
cn = cable needle;
cont = continue;
dec = decrease(ing);
foll = follow(s)(ing);
inc = increase(ing);
k = knit; **p** = purl;
patt = pattern;
rem = remain(ing);
rep = repeat;
RS = right side;
sl = slip; **st(s)** = stitch(es);
tog = together;
WS = wrong side
C4B = cable 4 back as foll: sl next 2 sts on to cn and leave at back of work, k2, then k 2 sts from cn
C6B = cable 6 back as foll: sl next 3 sts on to cn and leave at back of work, k3, then k 3 sts from cn
Cr4L = cross 4 left as foll: sl next 2 sts on to cn and leave at front of work, p2, then k 2 sts from cn
Cr4R = cross 4 right as foll: sl next 2 sts on to cn and leave at back of work, k2, then p 2 sts from cn
Tw2 = twist 2 as foll: k2tog without slipping sts from left-hand needle, then k first st again and sl both sts off needle tog

3rd row: P2, C4B, p6[6:10], Tw2, *p1, Cr4R, Cr4L, p1, Tw2, p6[10:10], Tw2, p2, k6, p2, Tw2, p6[10:10], Tw2, p1, Cr4R, Cr4L, p1*, Tw2, p6[6:10], C4B, p2.

4th row: K2, p4, k1, (p3tog, (k1, p1, k1) all in next st) 1[1:2] times, k1, p2, *k1, p2, k4, p2, k1, p2, k1, (p3tog, (k1, p1, k1) all in next st) 1[2:2] times, k1, p2, k2, p6, k2, p2, k1, ((k1, p1, k1) all in next st, p3tog) 1[2:2] times, k1, p2, k1, p2, k4, p2, k1*, p2, k1, ((k1, p1, k1) all in next st, p3tog) 1[1:2] times, k1, p4, k2.

5th row: P2, k4, p6[6:10], Tw2, *p1, k2, p4, k2, p1, Tw2, p6[10:10], Tw2, p2, k6, p2, Tw2, p6[10:10], Tw2, p1, k2, p4, k2, p1*, Tw2, p6[6:10], k4, p2.

6th row: K2, p4, k1, ((k1, p1, k1) all in next st, p3tog) 1[1:2] times, k1, p2, *k1, p2, k4, p2, k1, p2, k1, ((k1, p1, k1) all in next st, p3tog) 1[2:2] times, k1, p2, k2, p6, k2, p2, k1, (p3tog, (k1, p1, k1) all in next st) 1[2:2] times, k1, p2, k1, p2, k4, p2, k1*, p2, k1, (p3tog, (k1, p1, k1) all in next st) 1[1:2] times, k1, p4, k2.

7th row: P2, C4B, p6[6:10], Tw2, *p1, Cr4L, Cr4R, p1, Tw2, p6[10:10], Tw2, p2, k6, p2, Tw2, p6[10:10], Tw2, p1, Cr4L, Cr4R, p1*, Tw2, p6[6:10], C4B, p2.

8th row: K2, p4, k1, (p3tog, (k1, p1, k1) all in next st) 1[1:2] times, k1, p2, *k3, p4, k3, p2, k1, (p3tog, (k1, p1, k1) all in next

st) 1[2:2] times, k1, p2, k2, p6, k2, p2, k1, ((k1, p1, k1) all in next st, p3tog) 1[2:2] times, k1, p2, k3, p4, k3*, p2, k1, ((k1, p1, k1) all in next st, p3tog) 1[1:2] times, k1, p4, k2. These 8 rows form the patt.** Rep them 11[12:13] times more, then work 1st and 2nd rows again.

Shape shoulders:
Cast/bind off 20[23:25] sts, cut off yarn and sl centre 38[40:44] sts on to holder, rejoin yarn and cast/bind off rem 20[23:25] sts.

FRONT:
Work as given for Back to **. Rep them 9[10:11] times more, then work 1st and 2nd rows again.

Shape neck:
Next row: (RS) Patt 30[30:34] sts, p2tog, turn and leave rem sts.
Cont on these 31[31:35] sts for left neck.
Next row: (K1, p1) in next st, p3tog, patt to end. 30[30:34] sts.
Keeping patt correct, dec 1 st at neck edge on next 10[7:9] rows. 20[23:25] sts.
Patt 4[7:5] rows straight, ending after 2nd patt row. Cast/bind off.
With RS of work facing, sl centre 14[22:22] sts on to a holder, join in yarn at neck edge to rem 32[32:36] sts, p2tog, patt to end. Complete to match 1st side, reversing shapings.

SLEEVES:

With 5mm (no. 6/US 8) needles cast on 50 sts.
Foundation row: (WS) Foll instructions for 1st size, work
as Back foundation row from * to *.
Cont in patt as foll:

1st row: Foll instructions for 1st size, work as 1st row
of Back from * to *.

Cont working from * to * on each Back row in turn
until 8th patt row has been worked. Now keeping patt
correct and working inc sts into Back patt at sides,
inc 1 st at each end of next row and 6[7:8] foll 8th rows.
64[66:68] sts. Patt 9 rows straight, ending after 2nd patt
row. Cast/bind off.

NECKBAND:

Join right shoulder seam.

With 4mm (no. 8/US 6) needles and RS of work facing,
pick up and k 14[17:19] sts down left front neck, across
centre front sts k2, (p2, k2) 3[5:5] times, pick up and
k 14[17:19] sts up right front neck, across centre back
sts p 0[1:0], k2[2:1], (p2, k2) 9[9:10] times, p 0[1:2],
k0[0:1]. 80[96:104] sts.

Beg next row p2[k1:p1], cont in k2, p2 rib, work 9 rows
more. Cast/bind off loosely in rib.

 Making up

Join left shoulder and neckband seam. Sew in sleeves
approximately 13[14:15]cm/5[5½:6]in below shoulders.
Join side and sleeve seams.

Ballet shoe bag

Keep your ballet shoes safe in this stylish drawstring bag.

Trimmed with an intarsia bow motif, there's no mistaking that this drawstring bag in stocking/stockinette stitch is intended for a lucky young lady to carry and store her ballet shoes.

GETTING STARTED

 Bag is straightforward to make without shaping but working intarsia design takes some practise

Size:
Bag is 31cm wide x 36cm deep (12in x 14in)

How much yarn:
2 x 100g (3½oz) balls of Patons 100% Cotton DK, approx 210m (230 yards) per ball, in colour A
1 ball in each of colours B and C

Needles:
Pair of 4mm (no. 8/US 6) knitting needles

Tension/gauge:
22 sts and 30 rows measure 10cm (4in) square over st st on 4mm (no. 8/US 6) needles
IT IS ESSENTIAL TO WORK TO THE STATED TENSION/ GAUGE TO ACHIEVE SUCCESS

What you have to do:
Work throughout in stocking/stockinette stitch. Use intarsia techniques to work bow design from a chart on front of bag. Make eyelet holes in fabric for drawstring cords. Work cast/bound-off row in another colour to form a picot edging.

The Yarn
Patons 100% Cotton DK is a pure cotton yarn. It has a slight twist and subtle sheen that produces good-looking stocking/ stockinette stitch fabrics and it can be machine washed. There is a large range of attractive colours to choose from.

Abbreviations:
beg = beginning; **cm** = centimetre(s); **cont** = continue; **k** = knit; **p** = purl; **patt** = pattern; **rep** = repeat; **RS** = right side; **sl** = slip; **st(s)** = stitch(es); **st st** = stocking/stockinette stitch; **tog** = together; **WS** = wrong side; **yfwd** = yarn forward/yarn over to make a stitch

Note: When working in patt from chart, read odd-numbered (WS) rows from left to right and even-numbered (RS) rows from right to left. Use a separate small ball or length of yarn for each area of colour, and twist yarns tog on WS of work when changing colour to avoid a hole forming.

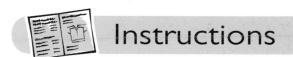 Instructions

BACK:
With A, cast on 70 sts.
Beg with a k row, cont in st st and work 96 rows, ending with a WS row.
** Eyelet-hole row: (RS) K2, *yfwd, k2tog, k2, rep from * to end.
Beg with a p row, work 10 rows in st st, ending with a RS row. Cut off A and join in B. P 1 row.
Picot cast/bind-off edging: (RS) Cast off 1 st, *sl st on right-hand needle back on to left-hand needle and cast on 1 st by inserting right-hand needle between first 2 sts on left-hand needle and drawing through a loop, place loop on left-hand needle, then cast/bind off next 3 sts, rep from * to end.

FRONT:

With A, cast on 70 sts.

Beg with a k row, cont in st st and work 15 rows, ending with a RS row. Now cont in st st and patt from chart until 61 rows from chart have been completed. Cont in A only and beg with a k row, work 20 more rows in st st, ending with a WS row. Complete as given for Back from ** to end.

 ## Making up

Press according to directions on ball band. With RS tog, backstitch along side and lower edges and turn RS out. With C, make 2 twisted cords, each 90cm (36in) long. With front of bag uppermost and beg at right side seam, thread one twisted cord through eyelets, ending back at right side seam. Tie ends tog and trim.

Now beg at left side seam, thread second twisted cord parallel to first through eyelets. Tie ends tog and trim. To close bag, pull both cords at the same time.

☐ A
■ B
▨ C

Little Miss Pink

Knit this doll and her clothes and make a cuddly toy
to treasure.

Who could resist this cute doll with beautiful flaxen hair? Her simple knitted body with integral vest is clothed in a skirt, bolero and shoes that are perfect for dressing-up play.

GETTING STARTED

 Doll and clothes are really simple to knit but take care with making up for a good finished effect

Size:

Doll is approximately 34cm (13½in) in height

How much yarn:

1 x 100g (3½oz) ball of Sirdar Bonus DK, approx 280m (306 yards) per ball, in each of five colours A – pink, B – flesh tone, C – bright pink, D – turquoise and E – primrose (pale yellow)

Needles:

Pair of 3mm (no. 11/US 2) knitting needles

Additional items:

3.mm (no. 11/US C) crochet hook

Stitch markers

Spare needle

Washable toy stuffing

Stranded embroidery thread in black, white, flesh tone and pink

Press stud (popper snap)

Tension/gauge:

25 sts and 24 rows measure 10cm (4in) square over st st on 3mm (no. 11/US 2) needles

IT IS ESSENTIAL TO WORK TO THE STATED TENSION /GAUGE TO ACHIEVE SUCCESS

What you have to do:

Work doll's body and clothes mainly in stocking/ stockinette stitch, using simple shaping. Work simple crochet edging around bolero. Add facial details with embroidery. Sew on strands of yarn as directed for hair and plait/braid.

The Yarn

Sirdar Bonus DK contains 100% acrylic. It is a good-value yarn that is ideal for toys as it can easily be machine washed and there are plenty of exciting colours to choose from.

Abbreviations:

alt = alternate;
beg = beginning;
cm = centimetre(s);
cont = continue;
dec = decrease;
foll = follow(s)(ing);
inc = increase;
k = knit;
m1 = make one stitch by picking up strand lying between needles and working into back of it;
p = purl;
psso = pass slipped stitch over;
rem = remain(ing);
rep = repeat;
RS = right side;
sl = slip; **st(s)** = stitch(es);
st st = stocking/stockinette stitch;
tog = together;
WS = wrong side

 # Instructions

DOLL:
BODY AND HEAD:

With A, cast on 53 sts. Place markers on 16th and 38th sts. Beg with a k row, work 32 rows in st st, ending with a WS row.

Next row: (RS) P to end.

Next row: K to end. Change to B and beg with a k row, work 2 rows in st st.

Shape shoulders:

Next row: K13, k2tog, k23, k2tog, k13. P 1 row.

Next row: K13, k2tog, k21, k2tog, k13. P 1 row.

Next row: k12, k2tog, k21, k2tog, k12. P 1 row.

Next row: K1, (k2tog) to last 2 sts, k2. 25 sts. Beg with a p row, work 3 rows in st st, placing markers at each end of 2nd row.

Shape head:

Next row: K1, (k1, m1) to last st, k1. 48 sts. P 1 row.

Next row: K13, m1, k22, m1, k13. P 1 row.

Next row: K13, m1, k1, m1, k22, m1, k1, m1, k13. 54 sts.

Beg with a p row, work 21 rows in st st, ending with a WS row.

Shape top of head:

Next row: (K2, k2tog) to last 2 sts, k2. 41 sts. P 1 row.

Next row: K1, (k2tog) to last 2 sts, k2. 22 sts. P 1 row.

Next row: (K2tog) to end. 11 sts.

Next row: (P2tog) to last st, p1.

Cut off yarn (leaving a long end for sewing up), thread through rem 6 sts and draw up tightly.

BODY BASE:

With A, cast on 10 sts. Beg with a k row, work 2 rows in st st. Cont in st st, cast on 2 sts at beg of next 4 rows. 18 sts.

Next row: Inc 1, k to last st, inc 1. 20 sts. P 1 row. Rep last 2 rows once more. 22 sts.

Work 2 rows straight.

Next row: Sl 1, k1, psso, k18, k2tog. 20 sts. P 1 row.

Next row: Sl 1, k1, psso, k16, k2tog. 18 sts. Cast/bind off 2 sts at beg of next 4 rows. 10 sts. Work 1 row. Cast/bind off.

LEGS: (Make 2)

With B, cast on 26 sts.

Beg with a k row, work 32 rows in st st, ending with a WS row.

Shape instep:

Next row: K16, turn.

Next row: P6, turn.

Working on these 6 sts only, work 8 rows in st st. Cut off yarn and leave sts on a spare needle. With RS of work facing, rejoin yarn at base of instep and pick up and k 7 sts down side of instep, k across 6 sts from spare needle, then pick up and k 7 sts up other side of instep and k across rem 10 sts. 40 sts. Work 3 rows in st st.

Shape sole:

Next row: K1, sl 1, k1, psso, k13, sl 1, k1,

psso, k4, k2tog, k13, k2tog, k1. 36 sts. P 1 row.
Next row: K1, sl 1, k1, psso, k12, sl 1, k1, psso, k2, k2tog, k12, k2tog, k1. 32 sts. P 1 row.
Next row: K1, (k2tog) to last st, k1. 17 sts.
P 1 row. Cast/bind off.

ARMS: (Make 2)
With B, cast on 6 sts.
Beg with a k row, cont in st st and work 2 rows.
Next row: K1, m1, k to last st, m1, k1. 8 sts.
Cont to inc 1 st in this way at each end of every foll alt row until there are 18 sts. Work 19 rows straight, ending with a WS row.

Shape hand:
Next row: K9, m1, k9. P 1 row.
Next row: K9, m1, k1, m1, k9. P 1 row.
Next row: K9, m1, k3, m1, k9. P 1 row.
Next row: K9, m1, k5, m1, k9. 25 sts. P 1 row.
Next row: K9, (sl 1, k1, psso) twice, (k2tog) twice, k8.
Next row: P8, (p2tog) twice, p9.
Next row: K9, k2tog, k8. P 1 row.

Next row: K1, sl 1, k1, psso, k4, (k2tog) twice, k4, k2tog, k1. P 1 row.
Next row: K1, (k2tog) to last st, k1.
Next row: (P2tog) 4 times. 4 sts.
Cut off yarn, thread through rem sts and draw up tightly.

SKIRT:
With C, cast on 186 sts. K 2 rows. Beg with a p row, work 17 rows in st st.
Next row: K1, (k2tog) to last st, k1. 94 sts.
Next row: P1, (p2tog) to last st, p1. 48 sts.
Next row: Cast on 2 sts, p to end. 50 sts.
Next row: Cast on 3 sts, k to end. 53 sts.
K 2 rows. Cast/bind off.

BOLERO:
BACK AND FRONTS:
(Worked in one piece to armholes)
With D, cast on 28 sts.
K 1 row. Beg with a p row, cont in st st, casting on 3 sts at beg of next 6 rows. 46 sts. Now inc 1 st at each end of every foll alt row until there are 52 sts, ending with a WS row.

Divide for armhole and Right front:
Next row: K10, turn.
Working on these 10 sts only, cont as foll:
Work 5 rows, dec 1 st at armhole edge of 2nd row and 1 st at each end of 4th row. Now dec 1 st at neck edge of next and every foll alt row until 3 sts rem, ending with a WS row. Cast/bind off.

Back:
With RS facing, rejoin yarn to rem sts, cast/bind off next 4 sts, k until there are 24 sts on right-hand needle, turn and cont as foll:
Dec 1 st at each end of foll 2 alt rows. 20 sts.
Work 9 rows straight. Cast/bind off.

Left front:
With RS facing, rejoin yarn to rem sts, cast/bind off 4 sts, k to end. 10 sts. Complete as given for Right front.

SLEEVES: (Make 2)
With C, cast on 24 sts.
P 1 row and k 1 row.
Cut off C and join in D. Beg with a k row, work 18 rows in st st. Cast/bind off 2 sts at beg of next 2 rows, then dec

1 st at each end of next and foll alt row. 16 sts.
Work 3 rows straight. Cast/bind off.

SHOES: (Make 2)

With D, cast on 30 sts. K 1 row.
Next row: P15, m1, p15.
Next row: K15, m1, k1, m1, k15. P 1 row.
Next row: K15, m1, k3, m1, k15. P 1 row.
Next row: K15, m1, k5, m1, k15. P 1 row.
Next row: K1, sl 1, k1, psso, k12, sl 1, k1, psso, k3, k2tog, k12, k2tog, k1. P 1 row.
Next row: K1, (k2tog) to last 2 sts, k2.
Next row: P1, p2tog, p4, (p2tog) twice, p4, p2tog, p1.
14 sts. Cast/bind off.

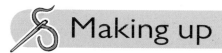 ## Making up

DOLL:

Join sole, heel and centre back seam of each leg and stuff firmly. Oversew cast on edges together. Join centre back seam of head and body, leaving bottom 4cm (1½in) open. Place tops of legs between markers at front of body, laying legs inside body piece. Pin body base to lower edge of body and backstitch through all thicknesses.

Turn to RS through opening. Stuff head firmly. Wind a length of B tightly around neck at markers and secure. Stuff body and close seam. Join underarm seam of arms and stuff firmly. Attach tops of arms to sides of body over shoulder shaping.

Cut approximately 50 x 65cm (25in) lengths of E for hair. Backstitch lengths into position, just to side of centre to form a side parting and from front to just beyond top of head. Smooth strands and gather at nape of neck, stitching to back of neck. Divide strands into three and plait/braid. Trim ends and tie in a bow with a length of A.

With black embroidery thread, work eyes in satin stitch and straight stitch eyelashes above each eye.

Work small white highlight in top corner of eyes. Using stem stitch, work nose in flesh tone thread and mouth in pink thread.

Vest strap: (Make 2)

With A, cast on 19 sts.
Cast/bind off. Place straps over each shoulder and catch to top of reverse st st at front and back.

SKIRT:

Join centre back seam of Skirt, leaving top 3cm (1½in) open. Sew a press stud (popper snap) to waistband where it overlaps.

BOLERO:

Join shoulder seams. Join sleeve seams, then sew into armholes.

Edging:

With 3mm (no. 11/US C) crochet hook, C and RS of work facing, work in double (US single) crochet around outer edges of bolero and sleeves. Join with a slip stitch into first double (US single) crochet and fasten off.

SHOES:

Join heel and sole seam.

Straps: (Make 2)

With D, cast on 11 sts.
Cast/bind off.
Place shoes on doll's feet and mark position of straps to hold shoes on. Sew one end of strap to top inside edge of shoe and the other overlapping outside edge, working a French knot in C to secure.

Index

Acknowledgements

Managing Editor: Clare Churly
Editors: Jane Ellis and Sarah Hoggett
Senior Art Editor: Juliette Norsworthy
Designer: Janis Utton
Production Controller: Allison Gonsalves